Faith Out Loud

A Cumberland Presbyterian
YOUTH RESOURCE
Volume 4, Quarter 1

Discipleship Ministry Team
Ministry Council
Cumberland Presbyterian Church

August 2014

8207 Traditional Place
Cordova (Memphis), Tennessee 38016

©2014 Discipleship Ministry Team

All Rights Reserved. No part of this book may be reproduced or transmitted in any form or by any means, electronic or mechanical, including photocopying, recording, or by any information storage or retrieval system, without permission in writing from the publisher with the single exception that purchase of this curriculum grants the purchaser the right to copy and distribute student handouts within each lesson for use in their local church. For information address Discipleship Ministry Team, Cumberland Presbyterian Center, 8207 Traditional Place, Cordova (Memphis), Tennessee, 38016-7414.

The Discipleship Ministry Team of the Ministry Council of the Cumberland Presbyterian Church is the successor organization to the Board of Christian Education of the Cumberland Presbyterian Church.

Funded, in part, by your contributions to Our United Outreach.

First Edition 2014

Published by The Discipleship Ministry Team, CPC
Memphis, Tennessee

ISBN-13: 978-0692275054
ISBN-10: 0692275053

We want to hear from you.
Please send your comments about this curriculum to
the Discipleship Ministry Team at faithoutloud@cumberland.org

OUR UNITED OUTREACH
Made Possible In Part By Your Tithe To Our United Outreach

Table of Contents

Curriculum Users Guide v

Lesson 1: Ruth and Naomi: Say Whatcha Mean, Mean Whatcha Say 1

Lesson 2: Leah and Rachel 11

Lesson 3: Rahab 19

Lesson 4: Potifer's Wife 33

Lesson 5: Miriam: There Are No Small Roles in God's Work 47

Lesson 6: Jephthah's Daughter: Our Words Have Consequences! 59

Lesson 7: Dorcas / Tabitha 67

Lesson 8: Hagar the Horrible? 81

Lesson 9: Bathsheba 93

Lesson 10: Jezebel: Me, Myself, and I 105

Lesson 11: Prisca / Priscilla 113

Lesson 12: Lydia 125

Lesson 13: Cumberland Presbyterian Women 137

Welcome to the Faith Out Loud curriculum!

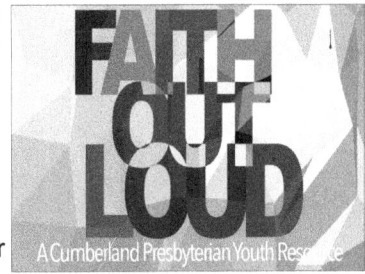

It is our prayer that these lessons both encourage you and equip you as a youth leader—we're so grateful for what you do in the lives of students!

Blessings to you and your ministry!

Below are explanations of the components found in each lesson and tips for using this curriculum.

Lesson Title: Each lesson has a catchy title. Use these titles as teasers to get your students excited about upcoming gatherings.

Scripture: Each lesson has a key scripture reference. Spend some time studying and praying through each week's passage as you prepare to teach.

Theme: The theme statement gives you a quick snapshot into the main point of the lesson.

Leader Prep: This section is usually divided into two parts: Resource List and Leader Prep. Resource List give you a quick list of all the stuff you need to gather for each week. Leader Prep give detailed instructions on the advance work that needs to be done for that week's activities. Do NOT wait until the night before you teach to review this section.

The Lesson: Once you move into the teaching time, you'll see these recurring elements:

- ✓ **Get Started:** These activities are designed to draw students into the material and set up the theme for the lesson.

- ✓ **Discussion Questions:** Usually a group of open-ended questions, these moments in the lesson are strategically placed to encourage your students to both think about and respond to the topic at hand.

- ✓ **Say:** Placed in italics, these sections can be read verbatim to your students to help them fully understand the implications of the topic or theme. You'll discover you'll get the best response when you are thoroughly familiar with these sections and can deliver the same information in your own words instead of just reading the info to the students.

- ✓ **Leader Tips:** You'll find sections of side notes throughout each lesson. These are notes just for you, the leader. These notes offer you everything from instructions on how to facilitate the activities to background information on the subject to tips for making your lesson run smoothly.

- ✓ **Listen Up:** This section highlights a key scripture passage that should be read aloud. Encourage student to do these readings as often as possible.

- ✓ **Now What:** This section helps your students respond to the lesson. This will drive the lesson home and get your students thinking about the lesson in terms outside of the classroom walls.

- ✓ **Live It:** This is simply just the closing of each lesson, designed to help you conclude your time with your students well and offer them something to think about in the week ahead. Most weeks have handouts to pass along to your students during this time. You may find it helpful to encourage your students to get a folder to keep these handouts together so they can easily refer to them during the week.

- ✓ **Handouts:** At the end of some lessons, you'll find a reproducible page. Your purchase of this curriculum grants you the right to print and distribute copies to everyone in your group.

- ✓ **Just in Case/Digging Deeper:** These provide opportunities to continue the lesson and enable further learning.

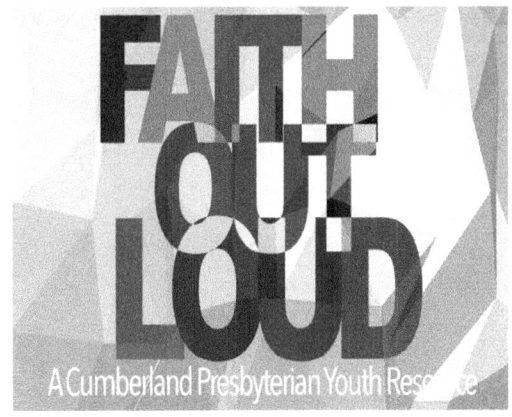

Ruth and Naomi
Say Whatcha Mean, Mean Whatcha Say
by Abby Prevost

Scripture: Ruth 1:16

Theme: Obedience and discernment are not always the easiest things to live out. God may tell us one thing but we desire another. Same with our actions and words, we say one thing but do another. Through this lesson we will explore what it means to be obedient, faithful, and loyal to God and Gods calling on our lives.

Resource List

- Music player (laptop, iPod, MP3 player, CD player, speakers, etc.)
- "I'll be there for you," by the Rembrandts along with lyrics
- Newsprint
- Markers
- Magazines
- Stickers
- Paint
- Scissors
- Various art supplies
- Bibles
- "You've Got A Friend," by James Taylor along with lyrics

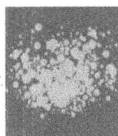

Leader Prep

- "I'll be there for you," by the Rembrandts along with lyrics
- "You've Got A Friend," by James Taylor along with lyrics

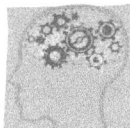

Leader Insight

Connecting to Your Students
As loneliness becomes the norm in today's society, it is no surprise that people are yearning for relationships. Our young people are no exception to this. Young people yearn for relationships with people who will be there for them. No matter what. And actually mean it. Whether the relationship is with parents, cousins, friends, coaches, teachers, grandparents, girlfriend/boyfriends etc., they desire the security of knowing someone will be there for them. Ultimately, we all yearn for these types of relationships; relationships where actions mirror the statement, "I'll be there for you no matter what."

As leaders who love and care for our students, we sometimes miss the how important it is that they know, through words

Notes:

and actions, we will be there to journey with them through whatever they encounter in their lives. We want to help them understand that just as they desire relationships with people who will be there for them, they to need to be willing to do the same for others.

Scripture provides us with a beautiful example of what this kind of relationship looks like with the story of Ruth and Naomi.

Explaining the Bible

Ruth is one of the most beloved women and stories of the Bible. Ruth was a Sojourner Truth of her time period. Despite the less than ideal times, she lived her life focused on inclusivity, obedience, and faithfulness to God, her family, and her promises.

In the opening of the book, we learn that Ruth's story takes place during the events in the book of Judges. This era is known for its bloody battles, hostility, divisions among the nations, and continued disobedience to God. We also learn that there was a famine in the land of Bethlehem in Judah. Ironically enough, the Hebrew meaning behind Bethlehem is "house of bread." (Ruth: The New Interpreter's Bible 833) Due to the famine in the land, Elimelek moved his family from Bethlehem in Judah to live in the country of Moab. The famine must have been extreme for Elimelek to move his family to a land where it was uncommon for the descendants of the two nations to commune. His family would create a life for themselves. Elimelek was married to Naomi, and they had two sons: Mahlon and Kilion. Moving from her homeland was just the beginning of the many sorrows Naomi would face. While living in the foreign country, Elimelek would die, Naomi's sons would marry Moabite women named Orpah and Ruth, and both Mahlon and Kilion would die. Thus, Naomi survived as a widow along with her two daughters in law. Being a widow during this time was terrible. Many times the women were taken advantage of, forgotten, marginalized, or simply ignored.

It was custom that the closest of kin to the deceased husband cared for the widow. So as if being a widow was not bad enough, Naomi being from Bethlehem of Judah had no family in Moab (besides Orpah & Ruth), and she couldn't even be sure she had any living relatives back in her homeland. Despite all the uncertainty she was facing, Naomi made the decision to return to her homeland. She encouraged her daughters in law, Orpah and Ruth, to return to their families so they could get on with their lives. Both Orpah and Ruth proclaimed that they wanted to stay with her. After Naomi pleaded the case that she could not bear any more sons to be their husbands, Orpah made the decision to return to her family. Ruth however, did not follow suit. She made the decision to stay with her mother-in-law. Despite efforts made by Naomi suggesting she stay in her country and return to family, Ruth stayed. Ruth proclaimed that she was not going to turn away from Naomi, her people, or her God, until God parted them in death.

When the two women return to Naomi's homeland, Naomi, which means "pleasant one," changes her name to Mara, which means "dealt bitterly." (Ruth: The New Interpreter's Bible 839) Obviously Naomi's (or Mara's) outlook on the world has changed significantly.

Ruth was a woman of her word, however. She listened to, learned from, cared for, and was faithful to Naomi. She trusted all that Naomi asked her to do—even lying down at Boaz's threshing floor. Boaz was the owner of the fields where Ruth had been gathering grain from; he was also close kin to Elimelek. By listening to the advice of Naomi, Boaz agreed to marry Ruth because he recognized her loyalty to the family.

After Boaz received the sandal of a closer kinsman, the two could be married. During this time period the exchanging of a sandal was to publicly confirm an agreement or transfer of property. Naomi was pleased with this arrangement because her family name lived on through Obed who would be the father of Jessie and the grandfather of David.

Within the book of Ruth, God does not have a speaking role, but God is far from absent from the story. There are two places in the book that refer to God: when Naomi learns the famine in her homeland is over and in Ruth's pregnancy. Both represent experiences that ancient Israelites believed to be beyond human control.

Ruth was an outsider during a time when she could have easily been discarded, but she did not let that stop her from staying loyal to her family and what God was calling her to do. God calls us all to be faithful, obedient followers.

Theological Underpinnings
Students will open the session by discussing what it means to stay loyal to your word and relationships. They will explore two sides of loyalty: how they have or have not stayed

Notes:

loyal, and how others have or have not stayed loyal to them. Through this exercise students will journey through what the phrase, "actions speaker louder than words" means. The goal is to help young people understand the loyalty that Ruth showed to Naomi both by word and actions.

Students will then work in groups putting together the story of Ruth for one another. By doing this they will learn of the various trying times Ruth and Naomi faced and how their loyalty, faithfulness, and obedience never waivered, no matter the circumstance. The students will gain an understanding of what it means to stay true to their promises. Students will end the session with a prayer asking God to help them be mindful of their words, actions, obedience, and faithfulness, not only to God but also to those around them.

Even though Ruth was a foreigner, her faith and selflessness earned her a place in the Holy Scriptures. Abraham believed, and it was credited to him as righteousness. Rahab the prostitute, and her whole family, was saved because of what she did for the two Israelite spies. Even though Ruth was a Moabite, she lived selflessly in accord with God's commandments. We must remember that the Creator's fingerprints are found on all God's children, whether they are part of the "in" crowd or not. Praise God that salvation and freedom is available for everyone!

Applying the Lesson to Your Own Life

As imperfect people, too many times we tend to say one thing and then do another. We are loyal to something or someone as long as it is convenient for us or we can gain something from it. Too many times loyalty stops once it is no longer convenient or there's nothing to gain. We can think of a cat who may be only sticking around because it's being fed.

As you prepare for this lesson, read the book of Ruth in its entirety. Think back throughout your life when someone said one thing but his or her actions said another thing. How did that make you feel you? Did you trust that person after that? Was it situational that they had to go back on their word? Also, think about times when you may have said one thing but done another. How do you think it made someone feel?

The Lesson

Get Started (10 min.)

As the students arrive, have "I'll Be There For You," by The Rembrandts, playing.

Begin by asking students if they paid attention to the words of the song playing as they entered. If no one can recall what they were hearing, state the chorus of the song:

> I'll be there for you (When the rain starts to pour)
> I'll be there for you (Like I've been there before)
> I'll be there for you (Cause you're there for me too)

Once you have gone over the chorus of the song, break students into groups and have them discuss and list: What it means to be there for someone, and a time in their lives when someone's actions did not mirror what they said.

Record their answers on newsprint. After a few minutes of brainstorming, bring the groups back together. Have each group share what they think it means to be there for someone and instances in their lives where someone's actions did not mirror what they said.

Discussion Questions:
- As we created these lists, were any feelings provoked? If so, what were they?
- How does it make you feel when people disappoint you?
- How do you react when someone disappoints you?
- Have you ever knowingly disappointed anyone? If so, how did it make you feel?
- Do you find it hard to forgive and trust someone who goes against his or her word?

Explain to your students that sometimes it is not a person's intention to let us down or go back on their word, but circumstances can occur that create difficult situations.

Discussion Questions:
- After considering this statement, do you think this is true for some of the instances we discussed earlier?

Notes:

Notes:

- If so, how do you think you would have felt if you had considered the actions circumstantial?
- Would it have made you feel and react differently? If so, explain.

Say: *Keep in mind all that we have discussed thus far because today's scripture shows us a lady who made a bold statement to her mother-in-law, and she provides for us a beautiful representation of a person saying what she meant, and meaning what she said.*

 ## Listen Up (25 min.)

Say: *Today we are going to be exploring the relationship between Ruth & Naomi. Ruth is known for her loyalty to her mother-in-law, Naomi. The book of Ruth is a short book of four chapters. We are going to refer to them as episodes.*

- Episode 1 (Ch.1)- Sorrow Strikes
- Episode 2 (Ch.2) Love Story
- Episode 3 (Ch. 3) The Proposal
- Episode 4 (Ch.4) Happily Ever After

Divide students into four groups, and assign each group one of the episodes. Have students read the assigned episode and summarize the events within it on newsprint. They may write words or phrases, draw pictures, summarize, create a poem or song, act out, or a mix any of these options.

Explain to students that they will be giving a summary of what they read to the entire group, so it is up to them to provide a good summary of their episode to help build the story together.

Have each group answer whether or not they think the episode (chapter) their group was assigned was given the correct title. If a group disagrees with the stated titled, have them explain why and what they think the title should be instead.

Once the allotted amount of time is up, ask the Episode 1

group to share their summary and whether or not they found the title of the episode fitting. Have the group hang their newsprint where everyone can see it. Have the other groups follow suit.

Discussion Questions:
- Why would Ruth make the choice to stay with Naomi after Naomi told her to return to her family?
- What do you think would have happened to Naomi if Ruth had not stayed with her?
- Do you think you could be as brave as Ruth? Why or why not?
- Do you think Naomi is thankful for all that Ruth did? Why or why not?
- In the book of Ruth, God does not have a speaking role, but is referenced when Naomi learns the famine in her homeland is over as well as when Ruth is pregnant. Where else did you see, hear, or feel God's presence in this story? Or did you think God seemed absent altogether?

Now What? (15 min.)

Tell the students to return to their groups of four. Distribute magazines, scissors, markers, paint, stickers, or a mixture of all to the different groups. Have students create something using those supplies that will serve as a reminder to them of what it means to be loyal, obedient, and faithful to God at all times. Once students have completed their item, bring them back together.

Say: *Earlier we discussed the importance of saying what you mean, and meaning what you say through words and actions. As we explored the story of Ruth and Naomi, we saw Ruth make a bold statement in verses 1:16-17: "But Ruth said, "Do not press me to leave you or to turn back from following you! Where you go, I will go; where you lodge, I will lodge; your people shall be my people, and your God my God. Where you die, I will die—there will I be buried. May the Lord do thus and so to me, and more as well, if even death parts me from you!"*

Notes:

Notes:

Discussion Questions:
- After learning the story of Ruth, does your idea/definition of being there for someone/being loyal to your word change? Why or why not?
- What are things we can do to strive to be like Ruth & Naomi?

 **Live It (5 min.)**

Display lyrics to the song "You've Got A Friend," by James Taylor. Tell the students to read and meditate on the lyrics as you play the song for them.

Once the song is over, ask your students to find a partner. After students have found a partner, ask them to share with one another prayer request and praises along with ways they can strive to be more loyal to the people around them and to God.

After students have finished praying, have them gather in a circle as you close with a prayer.

Say: *God, we say a lot of things; help us remember that our words and actions matter. Create in us a desire of unending loyalty, faithfulness, and obedience to you and those around us. When people we trust are disloyal to us, give us the strength to forgive. For it is from you that all blessings flow. Amen.*

© 2014 Discipleship Ministry Team of the Ministry Council of the Cumberland Presbyterian Church. All Rights Reserved.

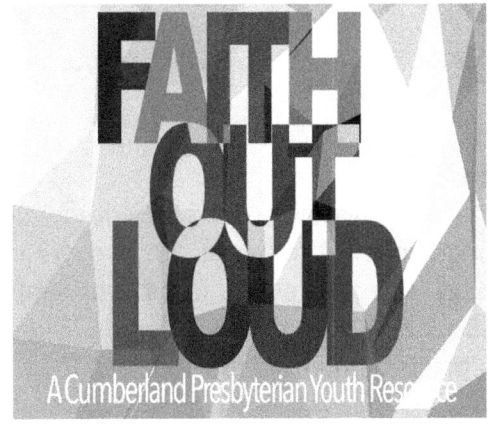

Leah and Rachel
by Taylor Young

Scripture: Genesis 29:15-30:22

Theme: God made each one of us with care and value, and comparing ourselves to each other only brings despair.

Resource List

- Paper
- Pens
- Note cards
- Magazines, newspapers, or pictures from the internet
- Bibles
- Glue
- Scissors

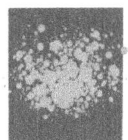

Leader Prep

- Set up a few chairs that will act as a talk show set for the drama activity.
- If you chose to do the alternate gathering activity, make sure to print out, or display, several pictures of unknown people (non-celebrities).

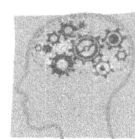

Leader Insight

Connecting to Your Students
Youth are in a world where they frequently have to weigh their value and worth based on the success and achievement of people around them. Students can even feel a pressure to succeed or live up to expectations from their own family members. Schools can encourage self-worth based on class rankings and award ceremonies for academic achievements. Youth who participate in band or sports are always viewed in comparison to someone who is considered "better than them," while they constantly compete with others for limited positions. Youth are particularly insecure during the developmental years, and this is an important time to develop a healthy and appropriate source of self-confidence that is countercultural to the competitive world that they are immersed in. The point of this lesson is to help them connect their value and worth to God's assigned identity, while the

Notes:

world around them assesses worth and value by temporary and superficial means.

Explaining the Bible

In this narrative, Jacob had previously deceived his father (Isaac) by disguising himself as his brother (Esau) in order to steal his brother's blessing. After this event, Jacob was sent away by his mother (Rebekah) to find his uncle Laban in order escape the wrath of his brother and to take a wife.

Jacob found Laban and fell in love with his youngest daughter, Rachel.

Jacob was made to work 7 years for Laban in order to marry Rachel. Laban deceived Jacob and was told he would have to marry Leah (who is described as less desirable) first. He then agreed to work for 7 more years to gain the hand of Rachel as well.

Our area of focus is the first mention of God in this narrative. The women are in competition to produce a male child for Jacob. This is important because the ability of a woman to produce offspring was her value in this society. It becomes a competition of worth for Rachel and Leah as they are trying to produce offspring for Jacob.

Upon marrying Jacob, Rachel found herself unable to have children, while Leah gave birth to four boys: Reuben, Simeon, Levi and Judah.

Desperate, Rachel asked Jacob to sleep with her maid Bilhah. It was a common practice for a man to sleep with a maidservant if the wife was unable to produce a male heir. Bilhah gave birth to two boys. Rachel named them Dan and Naphtali.

This only increased the rivalry between the two sisters. Leah asked Jacob to sleep with her maid Zilpah, and she too gave birth to two sons: Gad and Asher.

Leah decided to have more children with Jacob and gave birth to two boys and one girl: Issachar, Zebulun and Dinah (Genesis 30). Children were used as tools of revenge.

Finally Rachel gave birth to a son herself. He was called Joseph (Genesis 30:22-24).

God gives value to the least valued. This is an important

story for Christians to study. Even when Leah is described as less desirable, God showed her favor, and later, when Rachel is in distress because of her inability to produce an heir, God hears her supplications.

Theological Underpinnings

Being unified is one of the central theological components of This lesson will help youth understand the value God assigns them by first learning to recognize the worth of others. The first exercise will walk youth through the concept of seeing the value and worth of other people in order to accept it in their own lives.

Once they have taken a moment to see the value they have, they will see the way in which God loved and valued Rachel and Leah. Seeing God's interaction with people should provide the model for how they should outwardly act towards others.

They will then engage in a time of self-reflection to help them analyze the ways they may have undervalued themselves or others in every day life. Once they have reached this point, there will be a great opportunity to bring that deepened understanding of God's love and value for them back in to the world to show to others.

Finally, the students will practice meditative repetition for spiritual development by writing a prayer.

Applying the Lesson to Your Own Life

It is highly probable that there are aspects of your life that are held up in comparison to someone else or a certain standard. As a leader, what, or who, gives you value or worth? Christ has already overcome your weaknesses and declares you worthy! The story of Rachel and Leah can be a reminder of where are worth and value comes from. Always remember that biblical texts demonstrate the loving character of God, and this is no exception. Make sure to be transparent, and share your struggles with the youth that you are leading so that you spiritually grow together.

Notes:

Notes:

The Lesson

Get Started (12 min.)

Have students enter the room and simply write their name on the top of a notecard. Once they have done this, have them return the notecards to you.

Offer this word of welcome: *God has created each person in this room with wonderful aspects of God's own image. We thank God for God's creation. Today we are going to write about the great things we see in God's creation.*

Have the youth go around and say their names in the group in case there is anyone who does not know someone else in the group.

Prepare to distribute the notecards to the group. Warn them not to share the name on the notecard they get or let anyone else see it. Distribute the notecards making sure no one gets their own card. Be aware of any conflicts you may know of between students who will not say kind things about the person on the card.

Tell the youth that they have two minutes to write all the wonderful gifts that they have seen God give this person on their notecard. It could be their personality or the ways they've helped in the youth group. Warn them against writing any negative things about the other person.

Once the two minutes have passed, have them return the card to you. Make sure to mix them up, and then read each one of them aloud without disclosing the identity of the writer.

Discussion Questions:
- Why is it important to see aspects of God in other people?
- Tell me about something you feel God has gifted you with.

Say: *God has created us all with unique gifts and qualities that reflect God's own image. God knows your individual worth and value. Today we are going to look at Rachel and Leah—how they sought their value and worth in others, and how ultimately God showed how much he valued them.*

Alternative Option

Bring in magazines, newspapers, or pictures from the Internet of random people. Try not to get faces that youth will already know.

Offer this word of welcome: *God has created every person with unique gifts and cares about them very much. I want you to pick a photo and take 2-3 minutes, and make up a story about this person's life and the good thing God is doing with them.*

Then have each person come up and share their story of their person.

For larger groups, you could give one image to a group of 2-3 for them to share.

# Listen Up (20 min.)

Read aloud, or have someone read, Genesis 29:15-30:22.

Drama for the Baby Mommas!

Select up to five youth, and give them 10 minutes to read the passage above. Allow them time to rehearse and retell the story as if it were a modern-day talk show.

It might be fun to even have the guys play some of the girls, or whatever makes it more exciting for your group.

Assign roles:
Host (Maybe the God character)
Leah
Zilpah
Rachel
Bilhah

Say: *At this point in time, a woman's value in life was found in her ability to produce children. It is no wonder that Rachel*

Notes:

Leader Tip:
If you are dealing with a larger group, break them up in to smaller groups of 3-4 to have them share with one another.

and Leah were so desperate to do so. But what we see is that God loved and valued them both, regardless of their situation.

Now What? (20 min.)

Discussion Questions:
- Why would Leah and Rachel feel the need to compete with one another?
- How did God treat each of them?
- Ask each person to tell a story of when they felt like they were in competition with someone else?
  - Then, once they have shared their story, ask them to share how they think God views them and the person they were in competition with.

Prayer for Value

Have the kids develop a prayer that they can pray throughout their week to help them re-envision the way that they see their value and the value other people.

Give the kids magazines, newspapers, scissors, glue, and paper. Have the kids break up in to groups of 2-3 and cut out words and phrases to form a prayer. Once they have created them, have them save a photo on their cell phones to take with them.

For fun, you may want to have them add them to Instagram with a common hashtag for your youth group so they can all see them.

 ## Live It (5 min.)

Challenge the youth to pray this prayer each day of the week and revisit the prayers next week to check in.

Consider offering one of the prayers as a closing for your group or use this one: *Gracious God, the world calls me wotrthless and a sinner. But you redeem us. You give us worth. You value us as your children. Thank you. May we never forget the love you have for us.*

Consider closing with this prayer with a psalm.

© 2014 Discipleship Ministry Team of the Ministry Council of the Cumberland Presbyterian Church. All Rights Reserved.

Notes:

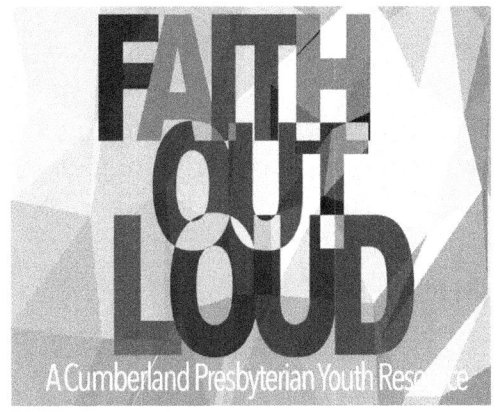

Rahab
by Andy McClung

Scripture: Joshua 2:1-6, 15-21, 6:22-23, Hebrews 11:29-31, and James 2:25-26

Theme: God can do good things through imperfect people.

Resource List

- Lots of red string suitable for making bracelets
- Several pairs of scissors
- Pads and pens
- Large sheet of newsprint or butcher paper, or large marker board
- Markers
- Enough space to split the class in two groups to work separately
- 1 photocopy of Group 1 handout
- 1 photocopy of Group 2 handout
- Two standard, letter-sized envelopes

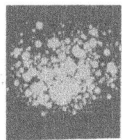

Leader Prep

- If you don't know how to braid string or make friendship bracelets, make sure one of your students does. If none do, find a guest to come to class and teach this, or search online and find instructions to print.
- If you don't normally have an assistant, this would be a good week to have some help.
- Seal each of the handout photocopies in its own envelope.

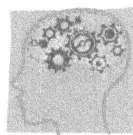

Leader Insight

Connecting to Your Students
While "no judgment" is a trendy attitude among teens today, people, including teens, still make snap-judgments of other people based on appearances, reputation, rumors, prejudices, biases, stereotypes, and other information. It's just human nature. Snap-judgments aren't always incorrect. It's actually amazing how the human mind can subconsciously perceive and process massive amounts of information in a quick glance. Instinct and intuition have saved countless lives and kept untold numbers of people away from dangerous people and situations.

When it comes to judging people, though, it's a problem

Notes:

Leader Tip:
The word "Rahab" is used in Job, Psalms, and Isaiah to refer to a sea monster, Egypt, and vanity/pride. This has nothing to do with the woman known as Rahab.

when we allow snap-judgments or preconceived ideas to override new information. Just because someone was weird in the third grade doesn't mean he's still weird in the tenth grade. Many people, including teens, hold on to outdated perceptions of people, judging them for who they used to be rather than who they are. The truth is, God often works through people with imperfect pasts, despite what we may think of them.

Explaining the Bible
After Moses died, Joshua took over leading the Israelites to the Promised Land. This land, however, was already occupied. That meant Joshua and the Israelites had to conquer it. Or, from their perspective, "take possession" of what was rightfully theirs. Joshua sent in a couple of spies to do some reconnaissance before the first invasion. The spies entered the city of Jericho, the first stronghold with a protective wall surrounding it. The spies stayed overnight in Rahab's house. When the spies' presence was discovered, Rahab hid them, misdirected the king's soldiers, and then helped them escape the city. In return, the Israelites promised to spare her and her household during the invasion. Rahab later joined the Israelites and married a Hebrew man named Salmon.

Rahab was a prostitute. There's no getting around, or sugar coating, that; the Bible says it plain and simple. What the Bible doesn't mention is that there were two kinds of prostitution in that culture: ones who walked the streets in such attire as to make it clear that they were willing to trade sex for money or food, and cultic prostitutes. This second kind of prostitute was a person, either male or female, who worked in a temple built to honor some pagan god or goddess. Worshipers of that god would pay to have sex with the prostitutes. In the minds of these worshipers and the leaders of these religions, such actions honored their god or goddess. Whichever kind of prostitute Rahab was, no Israelite would ever imagine such a person doing something good. We don't know which kind of prostitute Rahab was, but it is clear that she is meant to be the surprise hero of this story.

Reading Rahab's story raises some questions.

Just what were those Israelite spies doing in the house of a prostitute? The easily assumed answer is that they were doing what far too many people do today when out of town and away from their families. But maybe Rahab's house was a place where foreigners would easily blend in -- travelers would have been likely to visit a prostitute – and they wanted to be as inconspicuous as possible. Maybe they thought they could overhear some information that would help the invasion, either from civilians or from soldiers, who are traditionally associated with engaging the services of prostitutes. Maybe Rahab also ran an inn (the professions of innkeeper and prostitute could easily complement one another), and this inn had legitimate customers as well as those looking for a prostitute. Maybe Rahab ran a brothel, and the spies mistook it for an inn.

How did the king of Jericho know there were Israelite spies in town? This one is impossible to answer definitively.
Why did Rahab help the spies? This question is easier to answer than the others, since Joshua 2:8-12 says that Rahab somehow knew that the Hebrew God was powerful enough to achieve victory for the Israelites against Jericho and also willing to protect her and her family.

Why is Rahab considered a hero? Rahab could be seen as just a clever woman saving her own skin, but a deeper look reveals more. Prostitutes like Rahab are sinners, but they're also victims. In ancient societies, poor, single women had few ways to make money, and prostitution was a way to stay alive. This is still true in parts of the world today. Many prostitutes are forced into that life by alleged boyfriends for financial gain. Many women are kidnapped, enslaved, and prostituted out for financial gain. Prostitutes are frequently beaten or even killed by their customers. Without people (mostly men) willing to pay for sex, prostitution would not exist. So, while not always innocent, prostitutes are usually victims and outcasts. They are the very kind of people Jesus spent time with, which angered the religious leaders of his day. Besides assisting God's people in conquering Jericho, Rahab turned to God and rose above a life of prostitution. That's heroic. Additionally, she could have cut the deal only to save herself, but she made sure she included others, her family, in the deal. Thirdly, she chose faithfulness to God over loyalty to her country. That takes guts.

Theological Underpinnings
In Hebrews 11:31, Rahab is included in a list of people being praised for their strong faith. In James 2:25-26, Rahab is mentioned as an example to support the assertion that "faith without works is dead." So, was Rahab saved, both physically and spiritually, by something she did? The answer to that is a definitive, "sort of."

Some Christians believe that chooses ahead of time whom

Notes:

Notes:

will be saved. Others believe that it's up to the individual to accept Jesus for salvation. We Cumberland Presbyterians believe that the choice to accept Jesus is fully up to the individual, but we're only able to make a decision for Christ because God gives us the faith to do so. (See Confession of Faith 4.08.)

Rahab is a good model of the Cumberland Presbyterian position. God first reached out to her (we're never told exactly how) and showed her that he was God and that Jericho would fall to his chosen people—the Israelites. But Rahab still had to make the choice to turn her back on her old life and join God's people. In Joshua 2:11, she tells the spies, "The LORD your God is indeed God in heaven above and on earth below." By saying this, she's basically professing faith in the one, true, living God over and above any gods worshiped in Jericho. So, yes, Rahab had to do something to be saved, but God instigated the whole thing and gave her the faith to make that decision.

Applying the Lesson to Your Own Life
How quickly do you judge people based on appearance, stereotype, bias, or prejudice? What kind of snap-judgments are you more likely to make about people: positive or negative?

Would a prostitute (drug addict, criminal, etc.) feeling God's call to change his or her ways be welcomed in your congregation? Would you be one of those doing the welcoming?

Rahab assimilated into the Hebrew culture, but was always known as "Rahab, the prostitute," even though she apparently married, settled down, and changed her ways. Do you think her past was always a source of shame for her, or did she hold up her past to show God's power to change lives?

What's a negative thing in your past that you can't seem to shake? How might you think about that thing differently, to hold it up as an example of how God can change lives?

The Lesson

Get Started (15 min.)

Have your students choose the best artist among them, or you choose the best artist. (This person also needs to be someone who will behave him or herself while left alone for several minutes.) This person doesn't have to be a good artist, just the best in the class. You can send the person out of the room, or just make sure they don't hear what the class is saying.

Divide the rest of the class into two equal groups. If possible, have them work in separate rooms so they can't hear each other. Give each group a pad and pen, and have them designate a writer. Give each group one of the envelopes with the corresponding instructions in it.

This is where an assistant would be useful. Each group should work separately, preferably in different rooms, so neither group knows what the other is working on.

Allow the groups five minutes to work. Then call the whole class back together. Remind students not to mention what they were working on.

Have the artist rejoin the class and stand at the large newsprint or butcher paper.

Explain that the artist has no idea what the two groups were doing, but is going to draw a person based on descriptions given by the two groups.

Your artist may ask if he or she is supposed to be drawing a man or a woman. (Notice that neither group's instructions give any indication of gender.) If your artist asks, just tell them to do their best with the information given.

Have Group 1 read aloud one of their traits. Tell the artist to start drawing.

Taking turns, have the two groups read off their listed traits one-by-one. If the artist needs them to slow down, have them do so.

Notes:

Leader Tip:
If possible, arrange the artist's workspace in such a way that the class cannot see the progress. This is not necessary for the exercise, but it increases the fun of a big reveal when done.

Once all 20 traits have been read and the artist has included them in the drawing, have the artist step away.

Ask the artist to guess the person described. Ask Group 1 what they think Group 2 was told to describe. Ask Group 2 what they think Group 1 was told to describe.

If you had the artist drawing in secret, reveal the finished product now.

Point to the drawing, and say something like: *According to our descriptions, this is what a prostitute who's also a secret agent would look like.*

Pause so everyone can get a good look at the drawing, and either be amazed at the artwork or get a good laugh over it, whichever the case may be.

Transition into the lesson by saying something like: *The Bible tells the story of a woman named Rahab. She was both a prostitute and a secret agent.*

Listen Up (15 min.)

Have someone read aloud Joshua 2:1-6 and 15-21. This is a long passage, so you might consider dividing it among a few readers. Expect giggles over "Shittim."

Discussion Question:
- If God was on the Israelites' side and had already promised that they would conquer this territory, why would Joshua need to send spies to scout out Jericho? Why wouldn't he just march in with his army and take over?

Allow students to ponder and speculate on this, and then offer a possible answer. As we see throughout the Bible, God expects us to have faith, but God also expects us to gain knowledge, work hard, and take care of ourselves and others. That's what Joshua was doing. He had faith that God would give victory, but he did as much as he could to insure victory as well.

Besides, if the Israelites just marched in and destroyed Jericho, we never would have heard about Rahab. Because God revealed God's self and power to her, and because God insured her story was preserved in the Bible, God apparently wanted us to hear it.

Discussion Questions:
- In a story about spies sneaking into enemy territory to get information that will help an army to invade, who would you expect to be the hero?
- Who is the hero in this story?
- What does she do that's so memorable and heroic?

Explain that Jericho wasn't very big, probably only about six acres (about six football fields). It also had a wall around it to protect it from attacks. In fact, it probably had two walls—an inner wall and an outer wall separated by ten to fifteen feet.

Point out how parts of your town, or city, or neighborhood, or a nearby retail area or school (anything familiar to your students), has grown and spread over the years, covering more land. Then explain that a walled city can't grow like that because of the wall. So, as a walled city's population rose, homes were built on top of the walls. Beams of wood or stone were placed atop the two walls to span the gap and houses were built on top of those beams.

Atop the wall was probably the low-rent area of a walled city, farthest from the important "downtown" area and the first place to take a hit in an attack on the city. This is probably where Rahab's house was, which meant someone could climb down from her roof or outer windows and end up outside the city, even when the gates were closed and locked.

Discussion Question:
- So, if Rahab's house was on top of the wall, and the walls of Jericho fell down (6:20), then how could Joshua send the spies into her house to collect her and her family afterwards (6:22-23)?

Allow students to ponder and speculate on this for a while, and then offer a possible solution. If Jericho was six acres, then the wall around it would have been at least 2,000 feet long or a lot more depending on its shape. If you have a math whiz in class, let him or her work out some more pre-

Notes:

Notes:

cise numbers. The Bible just says the wall fell down flat. This could easily mean part of the wall, not thousands of feet of it. Rahab's house, then, could have been on part of the wall that didn't come tumbling down. But her house sure would have been a scary place to be during all that wall collapsing; so it's another indicator of her faith in God that she stayed put.

Depending on your class, you might want to ask the following questions. Don't spend much time discussing them, though. These are more for fun, a mental exercise.

Discussion Questions:
- Why do you think those spies were in a prostitute's house?
- How do you think the king of Jericho knew there were Israelite spies in town?

Do spend some time discussing the following question, though.
- Why do you think Rahab helped the spies?

Read aloud Joshua 2:8-12.

Share some of the thoughts from the background information above.

Final question for very brief discussion:
- How do you think Rahab's family felt about her profession?
- How do you think Rahab felt about her profession?

Transition to the next portion of the lesson by saying something like: *Rahab, a prostitute, saved those spies and helped the Israelites conquer the city. Afterwards she joined them, got married, and became a direct ancestor of King David, King Solomon, and -- through Joseph -- Jesus himself. God can do good things through imperfect people.*

Now What? (15 min.)

For this part of the lesson you'll need the red string and scissors. Students will make bracelets, necklaces, bookmarks, or just something to hang off a belt loop or keychain.

All the bracelets, etc. do not have to be identical. In fact, if it is at all possible, provide several different types of string. Embroidery floss is thin and shiny. Yarn and hemp cord are thick and rough. Silk cord is thick, shiny, and smooth. Leather strings and paracord are thick, strong, and more masculine. (No one making a bookmark should use leather or paracord. Those are too thick and will damage a book.)

If you or a student knows how to make survival bracelets from paracord, consider making these instead, especially if you think your students would be more excited about making these than friendship bracelets.

Hand out the string and scissors. Say something like: *The red string that Rahab hung out of her window can symbolize Rahab's faithfulness to God, and the Israelites' faithfulness in keeping their promise to her. It can also serve as a reminder that God can do good things through imperfect people.*

Explain that the class will now make bracelets out of red string. Have the student(s) who know how to make the bracelets teach the others. Each student is to make two bracelets. If anybody asks why they're making two, just say that it will be explained later.

While students work, say something like: *What Rahab did was never forgotten by the Israelites. About 1,400 years later, they were still talking about how faithful she was.* Then read aloud Hebrews 11:29-31, and James 2:25-26.

Leader Tip:
If you're worried about having enough time for this lesson, and if you think your students can weave during the discussion, start making the bracelets during the "Listen Up" portion of this lesson.

Just In Case:
It's tough to hear the story of Rahab and not wonder about God's people completely destroying a city and its populace, supposedly on God's command. If a student asks about this, you can say something like, "That's something that troubles me too, but this lesson isn't about that. Maybe we can talk about that some other time. Right now, let's focus on what we can learn from Rahab's story."

DIGGING DEEPER

An immoral woman with a heart of gold is a stereotypical character that shows up frequently in fiction and myths. Sometimes she's a prostitute, sometimes a stripper, sometimes just a "loose" woman. A few examples: Jamie Lee Curtis' character in Trading Places (1983), Julia Roberts' character in Pretty Woman (1990), Vivica Fox's character in Independence Day (1996), Ros from Game of Thrones, Heather Graham's character from The Hangover (2009). Rahab, a prostitute who does something significantly good, may be the source of this recurring character. Most real-life prostitutes, however, are selling sex either 1) to survive, 2) because they're forced to, or 3) to support a drug habit. That's tragic, not glamorous or heart-warming.

Just In Case:

It's tough to hear the story of Rahab and not wonder about God's people completely destroying a city and its populace, supposedly on God's command. If a student asks about this, you can say something like, "That's something that troubles me too, but this lesson isn't about that. Maybe we can talk about that some other time. Right now, let's focus on what we can learn from Rahab's story."

Live It (5 min.)

Ask each student to hold up the two items they have just made out of red string.

Say: *None of us is perfect. One of those bracelets is for you. Wear it, or carry it in your pocket. Let it remind you that God can do good things through imperfect people.*

Also say: *Someone you know, or will meet, may feel useless to God because they're not perfect. Maybe they've done something bad in the past. Your second bracelet is for that person. Give it to them, tell them Rahab's story, and assure them that God can do good things through imperfect people.*

Resources used: All the Women of the Bible, by Herbert Lockyer. friendship-bracelets.net. Helpmates, Harlots, and Heroes, by Alice Ogden Bellis. The Interpreter's Bible Vol. II.

© 2014 Discipleship Ministry Team of the Ministry Council of the Cumberland Presbyterian Church. All Rights Reserved.

GROUP 1 INSTRUCTIONS

As a team, come up with a ten-point list to describe a prostitute. You may brainstorm as many traits, characteristics, and descriptive features as you wish, but agree on just ten to write below and bring back to the whole class.

DO NOT describe a character from some Hollywood movie in which the prostitute is really a sweet person with whom the audience is supposed to fall in love. Describe a real-life, street-walking prostitute.

If you don't know what such a person would be like or look like, use your imagination.

You have five minutes. When you re-gather with the whole class, do not mention what you worked on.

1. _____
2. _____
3. _____
4. _____
5. _____
6. _____
7. _____
8. _____
9. _____
10. _____

GROUP 2 INSTRUCTIONS

As a team, come up with a ten-point list to describe a secret agent. You may brainstorm as many traits, characteristics, and descriptive features as you wish, but agree on just ten to write below and bring back to the whole class.

DO NOT describe a character from some Hollywood movie in which the secret agent is super-cool and gorgeous. Describe a real-life secret agent.

If you don't know what such a person would be like or look like, use your imagination.

You have five minutes. When you re-gather with the whole class, do not mention what you worked on.

1. _____
2. _____
3. _____
4. _____
5. _____
6. _____
7. _____
8. _____
9. _____
10. _____

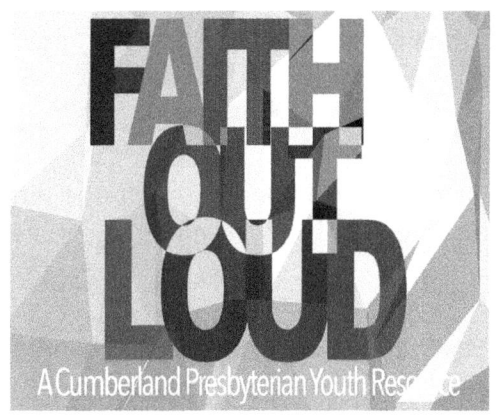

Potifer's Wife
by Andy McClung

Scripture: Genesis 39

Theme: A close relationship with God enables us to resist temptation.

Resource List

- (Optional) A chair for each student
- Enough space to gather students in a wide circle
- YouTube videos as listed in the "Getting Started" section of the lesson
- Video capability (laptop, projector, DVD player, speakers, etc.)

Leader Prep

- (Optional) Prepare printed handouts of Genesis 39, one per student
- Think back over the last six months or so of national and local news to recall some prominent reports of men accused of sexual misconduct

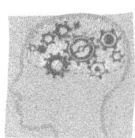

Leader Insight

Connecting to Your Students

Sex is on your students' minds... a lot. How could it not be? Already full of raging adolescent hormones, most of the advertisements, songs, TV shows, movies, and media images they're exposed to stir up those hormones even more. Just because sex is on their minds, however, doesn't mean they want to talk about it with you! Be sensitive to this, but don't shy away from the topic. The more comfortable you appear to be while talking about sex and sexuality in the classroom, the more comfortable, open, and honest your students are likely to be.

Learning appropriate uses of sex and sexuality is an important part of being a Christian, especially in a hyper-sexualized society. Cut your students some slack during this lesson if they use words you think are inappropriate; a shocked or disap-

Notes:

Leader Tip:
We usually focus on the Ten Commandments, but there were 613 points in Jewish law.

proving reaction to what they consider a benign word may close down honest communication.

Explaining the Bible

Potiphar's wife plays a tiny role in just one scene of one major Biblical character's life story, but she is well remembered for her actions.

Joseph's brothers, jealous that he was their father's favorite, handed him over to some slave traders and led dear old Jacob to believe that his favorite son had been killed by a wild animal. Joseph ended up in Egypt as a slave to Potiphar, a military man who was in charge of the Pharaoh's (Egyptian king) bodyguards, and possibly the whole Egyptian military. Potiphar recognized that God blessed everything Joseph did and made Joseph his business manager. Under Joseph's management, Potiphar's wealth grew, and his personal and business affairs ran smoothly.

And that's where Potiphar's wife comes into the story. This part wasn't so smooth.

Potiphar's wife is not the only woman mentioned in the Bible to misuse sex or her sexuality. She is, however, one of the few who seems to have no ulterior motive for her misuse of sex. She's not trying to trick anybody or avert a war or gain information or keep food on the table. Apparently, she just wants to have sex with Joseph.

The story of Potiphar's wife and Joseph was also not the first to include a wicked woman trying to seduce a stalwart, righteous man, nor was it the last. In fact, this is a common plot in myths and folklore. This leads some to say that that this story never really happened, that the Hebrew people adopted a common story and adapted it to showcase their hero, Joseph, as a righteous man.

Joseph does indeed come across as righteous in this story. And Potiphar's wife does indeed come across as wicked. But notice that she is not really judged within the narrative. Even Joseph, who loses his plush life and goes to prison because of her accusation, doesn't condemn her. The only thing he calls "wicked" is betraying someone who puts trust in you and committing adultery (verse 9). Perhaps this is a lesson for the many Christians today who seem to think that God has called them to a vocation of pointing out everyone else's sins.

It may be interesting for some to speculate why Potiphar's

wife was attracted to Joseph. We know he was handsome and physically attractive (verse 6), but we have to wonder if there was something more. Was it because he was so successful as a manager? Was it because "the Lord was with him" (verse 3) and she was drawn to that, but maybe she only knew how to relate to a man sexually? Was it because Joseph was a foreigner and she liked the idea of sex with an exotic man? Was is that she was rich, entitled, spoiled, and accustomed to getting what she wanted, when she wanted it, and never mind the consequences? Did she try to seduce everybody, and we only know about this one attempt because Joseph was the only one who refused? Was her husband sexually neglecting her? Was she trying to punish her husband for something by attempting to have sex with Joseph, his most trusted servant/slave/employee? Was she so bored (and cruel) that she was just trying to stir up trouble so she could watch the drama unfold, like some ancient soap opera, reality show hybrid? Well, speculate as we might, we can't know for sure.

What we do know is that her attempted manipulation of Joseph's life was meant for evil, but God used it for good. Because God was with him, Joseph ended up making connections in that prison—connections that would eventually put him pretty much in charge of all of Egypt.

Some of your students may have read Harper Lee's classic, To Kill a Mockingbird. If so, they may remember that a character in that novel, a Caucasian woman, falsely accuses an African-American man of rape when in fact she had made sexual advances on him, and he refused to respond. Perhaps Ms. Lee had this story of Potiphar's wife and Joseph in mind as she wrote. In both stories the reader has to notice some discordance in the sexually aggressive woman's behavior. She is attracted to a man of another race, but when rejected, in order to give her false accusation a better chance of being believed, she easily exploits the cultural prejudice of people like herself against people like the man who rejected her. Doesn't that seem to make a wicked woman even more evil?

Theological Underpinnings
The reason this story was told and retold by the Hebrew people, and then finally written down and preserved for all cultures for all time, had little to do with Potiphar's wife and a lot to do with Joseph's faithfulness to God. Although this incident occurred long before God included, "Don't commit adultery" in the Ten Commandments, anybody who knew God knew that it was wrong to have sex outside of marriage (since sex pretty much signified marriage in God's eyes).

Notes:

Notes:

Some preachers or teachers may zero in on the part of this story where the Bible says that God made everything Joseph did prosper, and then go from there to preach or teach that if we are as faithful as Joseph God will reward us and make sure we prosper too. That's questionable theology and hardly the point of this story.

The most important lesson for contemporary Christians to learn from this story is about temptation. Because we're looking at this story within this series of lessons, we have to pay attention to Potiphar's wife: she's more than just a literary device used to showcase Joseph's righteousness.

The theological lesson behind this story is about sexual temptation. Potiphar's wife was tempted to have sex with Joseph even though she was married. We can imagine that Potiphar's wife may have also been tempting for Joseph. But Joseph, on the other hand, resisted the temptation to have sex with her, while Potiphar's wife continually pushed him to sleep with her. What was the difference between them? What allowed Joseph to resist temptation when Potiphar's wife apparently didn't even try to resist? The answer is clear: Joseph sought to do what pleased God. Potiphar's wife sought to do what pleased her.

A side lesson learned from this story is that temptations may increase in the lives of those who follow God, coming either from Satan or from people who want to drag down righteous people because of their own guilt from their sin.

Applying the Lesson to Your Own Life

Potiphar's wife doesn't tease, bat her eyelashes, drop hints, or send mixed messages. She just comes out and says that she wants to have sex with Joseph. What were you raised to think — that girls should never ask out a boy, or it's a woman's right to make her interest known? Do you still hold on to those teachings, or have you changed?

Do you think advertisements, movies, TV, and music make it harder for people today to resist sexual temptation? If so, what can you do about it?

Are you comfortable or uncomfortable talking about sex in church? Why?

What constantly tempts you? What's your greatest help in resisting temptation? What factor, when present, is likely to insure that you will not be able to resist temptation? How do you feel after resisting temptation? How do you feel after failing to resist?

The Lesson

Get Started (10 min.)

Option #1

If you have the ability to show YouTube videos in class, choose some of the following. Show them to your students, and then discuss the questions below.
- "Las Vegas Commercial," (:31) posted by Andrew Komosa (This one has dated references your student may not understand.)
- "TV Commercial - Visit Las Vegas - You Coming? - What Happens Here, Stays Here," (:31) posted by CommercialLand
- "What Happens in Vegas…," (:31) posted by videokidoe
- "Only Vegas 'What happens here, stays here' commercial – Jobs," (:31) posted by cellulove
- "What Happens in Vegas-'Pearly Gates,'" (:31) posted by Alison Burnmeister
- "What Happens in Vegas-'Reason,'" (:31) posted by Alison Burnmeister

Discussion Questions:
- What message do you think these commercials are trying to send?
- What is your response to that message?
- Does morality – what's right and wrong behavior in God's eyes – change when you're away from home? Or not in church?

Transition to the lesson by saying something like:
In the Bible, we find the story of Joseph, who is far away from home. When a woman tried to get him to do something he knew was wrong, Joseph could have done it and blamed it on

Notes:

Notes:

Notes:

the woman, on what was normal for the place they were in, or anything else. But instead he chose not to change his morals just because of where he was. He knew it would hurt his relationship with God and bring trouble.

Option #2

Question for the girls:
- Do you think girls sometimes use sex -- including flirtatious attention, kissing, or the promise of sex (even if just an implied, but not stated, promise)-- to get a guy to do something for them?

Question for the guys:
- Do you think guys sometimes do something for a girl because either she implied, she said, or he assumed that she would give him some kind of sexual reward, including flirtatious attention, kissing, or more serious stuff?

Question for both genders:
- Estimate how many different men you have seen in the news accused of some kind of inappropriate sexual activity. (Pause here for a number. Help your students remember some recent cases. Names of the accused aren't important.) Of those cases, do you remember how they ended – how many of those men were found not guilty, and how many were found guilty? (Presumably, your students will remember far more accusations than outcomes.)

Transition to the lesson by saying something like:
Because of how the news media reports things, an accusation of sexual misconduct is all it takes to ruin a man's career, making it difficult for him to feed his family and keep a roof over his head. Some women make false accusations as jokes, pranks, out of spite, or as revenge for something. But making a false accusation of rape or sexual assault is no joke. In fact, it's illegal.

In Genesis we find the story of Joseph who was falsely accused of attempted rape. He could have been killed over it but only ended up in prison.

Listen Up (20 min.)

Remind students of Joseph's story before Genesis 39 Then have students read Chapter 39 aloud and straight through. Warn them, however, that you will interrupt to explain some things along the way.

Since this is a long passage, have several students ready to read

A good way to break up the reading is
- Verses 1-6a
- Verses 6b-10
- Verses 11-18
- Verses 19-23.

It would be best to use an easily read, and easily understood, version of the Bible. If your students do not all have the same translation, consider photocopying Chapter 39, or printing copies of it from a website such as biblegateway.com and giving everyone a copy.

As students read, interrupt the reading in the following places to make the following explanations. Allow questions for clarification during the reading, but save discussions until after the entire chapter has been read.

- After verse 1, explain that "the captain of the guard" was a military man—either the top officer or the chief of the king's/pharaoh's bodyguards, or both.
- After verse 6, explain that, just like rock stars, movie stars, business moguls, and politicians today, the rich and noble people in the ancient world often hired someone to manage their business and finances.
- After verse 9, point out that while Joseph appreciated and respected the trust Potiphar had placed in him, the core reason he refuses Potiphar's wife's advances was because he thought adultery was wrong.
- After verse 10, point out that Potiphar's wife didn't "come on" to Joseph once or twice, but repeatedly.
- After verse 12, point out that if she had been coming on to Joseph repeatedly, but this was the first time they were alone, then someone else must have been close by all the other times; this may indicate that Potiphar's wife got excited by the danger of being caught.

Notes:

Notes:

- After verse 15, point out: 1) that the word translated here as "insult" or "mock" or "seduce" or "make sport" is used elsewhere (Genesis 26:8) to indicate a man touching a woman in such a way that an observer knew they were married; and 2) that Potiphar's wife is playing the "race card" by using the fact that Joseph is an alien/immigrant to get folks on her side and help sell her lie.

When the entire chapter has been read, invite discussion based on the following questions:
- To the girls: What do you think of a woman who is sexually aggressive like Potiphar's wife?
- To the guys: What do you think of a woman who is sexually aggressive like Potiphar's wife?
- Potiphar's wife lived in a place where she had everything she could possibly need, but she wanted the one thing forbidden to her. To get it, she would have to convince a man to do something against God's wishes. Does that sound familiar? (Similar to the story of Adam and Eve, perhaps?)
- Do you think Potiphar's wife was surprised by Joseph's initial refusal? If so, why?
- Have you ever been in a situation where you did what you knew was the right thing to do, and that confused somebody else? Why do you think they were confused?
- Do you think Joseph was tempted to say "yes" to her?
- She was tempted to have sex with him and failed to resist that temptation. He was presumably tempted to accept her invitation, but resisted that temptation. What did he have that she didn't, that allowed him to resist what she couldn't? Or why would he run away? (Affirm all serious answers, but you really want your students to understand here that Joseph's reliance on God and respect for God helped him say "No.")
- Why do you think Potiphar's wife lied?
- Potiphar's wife played the race card. Is it easier to believe someone of another race is guilty of a crime?
- Legally, Potiphar would have been justified in killing Joseph. Why do you think Potiphar threw Joseph in prison instead of killing him?
- Are there other things, besides romance, that try to seduce us, or tempt us to turn away from what we know God says is right?
- What makes it easier to resist temptation? What makes it harder?

Now What? (15 min.)

For this part of the lesson, you'll read a story about temptation. Students will stand up initially, and while you are reading, sit down when they think they would give into the temptation. Stop reading when the last student sits, regardless of where you are in the story.

Arrange chairs in a circle, facing out so students can't easily see each other. Have each student stand in front of a chair. You'll read from the middle of the circle. To play without chairs, have the students sit down on the floor at the appropriate time.

Emphasize that this isn't a competition to see who remains standing the longest or who sits down first, but rather an exercise to help the students think through what they would do before they ever get into a real situation of temptation.

Say: *I'm going to tell you a story. Imagine yourself in the story, being tempted to do something wrong. When you think the temptation for you would be too strong to resist anymore, sit down.*

Tell the story: *Your parents tell you that you are going to be home alone until really late Friday night. They say you have to come straight home after school, you can't go to the game Friday night, and nobody is to come over.*

You and the person you're dating had already planned to go to the game and then out for pizza with a bunch of friends. You tell yourself, "There's no need to break that date. My parents will never know."

At the game, several of your friends say they won't be joining you for pizza after all. This leaves just you and your date, and one other dating couple. You figure that will be okay and you all ride together to the restaurant.

During the end of the meal, the other couple asks if it'd be okay if they caught a ride with some other friends. You say, "Sure."

After the meal you still have a couple of hours before your date's parents expect him/her to be home. You think about

Notes:

Leader Tip:
There's nothing wrong with being uncomfortable. But if you think your students would be so uncomfortable using a sexually-themed story that the point of the exercise would be completely lost, use the alternate exercise, "The Party." Simply substitute the stories.

Just In Case:

A student may say – possibly joking, possibly not – that maybe Joseph was able to resist the temptation to have sex with Potiphar's wife because she was unattractive. If so, point out what we know about Potiphar and, more subtly, what we can conclude from that information. Potiphar was rich, and therefore would have been able to afford nutritious food, the best health care, the fanciest clothes, and the best cosmetics available. Would that make his wife more or less likely to be healthy and attractive? Potiphar was socially powerful, since he was so close to the king. He was a warrior, so he would have been athletically built. Would a rich, powerful, muscular man be more likely to have an attractive or an unattractive wife? Chances are Potiphar's wife was attractive. But if this question comes up, lead your students to draw their own conclusions about her level of attractiveness.

---

your empty house and how it's going to be empty for several more hours. You tell yourself, "We can just drive around for a while."

Driving around takes you near your neighborhood. You tell yourself, "We can just drive down my street. We won't stop." On your street, in front of your house, you decide to pull into the driveway. The driveway is dark. Nobody is around. You tell yourself, "We'll just stay in the car and talk. We won't go inside or anything."

Talking turns into kissing. You tell yourself that's all you'll do. It's a little bit cold outside so you decide to go inside. You tell yourself, "It's just to be more comfortable. We won't do anything more than kissing."

On the couch you start kissing again. Then hands start to roam. Your date suggests the two of you go to your bedroom. You tell yourself, "It's just to be more comfortable. We won't do anything more than kissing."

In the bedroom, clothes start to come off, but you tell yourself you're not going to go all the way.

Then your date says, "Let's go all the way."

If you've made it to the end of the story, pause for a moment before continuing with the lesson. Then ask a student or two to tell the others when they sat down, and why. If you have a small class, you can probably ask everyone. This is not a time for questions or judgment, but a time for listening to your students' ideas about temptation.

Ask a few students to tell how their story would end, based on where in the story they sat down. Again, if you have a small enough class, you can have everyone do this. If you have a large class, try to choose different students to explain when and why they sat down, and to finish their story.

This is a time for students to talk, not you. Don't give advice, praise, scold, or tell students they're fooling themselves. If you have enough time, however, and it feels right, do consider asking some helpful questions. "Is it easy or hard to resist that temptation?" "Are you good at resisting temptation?" "So that's not really a temptation for you?" "Why isn't that a temptation for you when it is for so many other people your age?" "Have you been able to resist that kind of temptation before? What helped? What made it harder?" "Have you ever put someone in a tempting situation?" "How did you feel afterward?" "Is it a good idea to stay in temptation, even if you feel you can overcome it?" "Who would have been Potiphar's wife in this story?" Who would have been Joseph?"

 ## Live It (5 min.)

Close the lesson with the following or a similar prayer: God, keep us from tempting others like Potiphar's wife did. Keep us from lying about others like she did. Help people like her learn to treat others better. Be with us, and keep us close to you so that we can resist temptation like Joseph.

Resources used: All the Women of the Bible, by Edith Deen. The Interpreter's Bible Vol. 1.

© 2014 Discipleship Ministry Team of the Ministry Council of the Cumberland Presbyterian Church. All Rights Reserved.

DIGGING DEEPER

Running Potiphar's house would have been quite a job. Potiphar would have been gone a lot. The house itself would have been big and elegant, needing cleaning and maintenance. There were probably several other servants and slaves to manage and direct. There would have been stables, horses, other animals, and all the associated gear to tend and store. Chariots were likely present, which would also need maintenance and storage space. There could have been fields and crops, or at least food storage. Someone had to go shopping. Someone had to handle the money for the shopping. Houseplants needed to be watered. Important guests had to be welcomed and pampered. To handle all of this, and handle it well, Joseph had to be smart, organized, a good leader, and good at multi-tasking.

ALTERNATE EXERCISE: THE PARTY

Tell this story: You hear that there's going to be a party after Friday night's game. There will not be any adults there. There will be alcohol and drugs. Everybody who goes to this party will get a boost in their popularity. You would like to be more popular, but don't like the idea of drugs being there. You decide not to go to the party.

After the game Friday night, you take the long way home—the way that goes right past the house where the party is. You tell yourself, "I'll just drive by; I won't stop."

You pull over when you see all the cars of the party-goers. You tell yourself, "I'll just stay in the car and see who goes in."
After a while you think, "I'll just go in for a few minutes to see who's here."

After getting inside, you think, "I'll take a look to see what kind of stuff people are doing. I won't drink anything or take anything."

After seeing the keg and the table covered with alcohol bottles and mixers, you tell yourself, "I'll just pour a drink so I'm not the only one without a cup in my hand. But I won't drink any of it."

After a while holding that cup, you think, "I look stupid just holding this cup. I'll just have this one drink. I won't get drunk."

After the cup is empty, you decide, "I'll fill it up again, so I'm not walking around with an empty cup, but I won't drink any of this one."

After a few drinks, someone offers you a pill, saying it's really good stuff. You know your decision-making abilities are not at their best anymore. So you tell yourself you'll accept the pill, just to be polite, but won't swallow it.

Miriam
There Are No Small Roles in God's Work
by Chris Warren

Scripture: Exodus 2:1-10, Exodus 15:20
Numbers 12, Numbers 20:1

Theme: Miriam, the sister of Moses and Aaron, may not be the most recognized character in the journey to the promised land, but Miriam was instrumental in God's work with the Israelites.

Resource List

- Percussion instruments (tambourines, small cymbals, castanets, shakers, and other small noisemakers)
- Handout "Miriam's Life" for each student

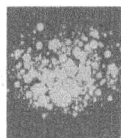

Leader Prep

- If you do not have percussion instruments, take time to create some together with your class.

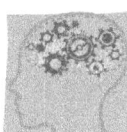

Leader Insight

Connecting to Your Students
Not everyone can be the most outstanding student, the best athlete, or the star of the school play. Actually, few people can have these honors. In our society we tend to imagine that being number one is the only worthy goal. There is a saying, "Second place is just the first loser." But that is not how we should rate people.

Sometimes we have the starring role in a certain situation, and sometimes we are in the background. This lesson is intended to help us recognize how God works through those in the background, or those less recognized than the stars. Miriam's work allowed Moses to do the work he did. When Miriam and Aaron became jealous of Moses' place, God explained that Moses was in a class by himself. Miriam's life, however, was still very important for the liberation of the Israelites.

Notes:

Explaining the Bible

Miriam is not mentioned in scripture very many times. Aside from the scriptures chosen for this lesson, Miriam is listed in a genealogy as an example in Deuteronomy (Remember what God did to Miriam when she got too proud?), and as an example of being sent by God in the book of Micah. Although Miriam was not the main player in the book of Exodus, she was instrumental in getting Moses where he needed to be; in helping to motivate the Israelites in battle against the Egyptians at the Sea of Reeds (commonly translated as "Red Sea"); and later leading the celebrations after the victory; and was considered by the people and God to be a prophet of the Lord.

In the first scene of Moses' life, just after he is born, Miriam is likely the sister referred to in scripture who watched as the basket drifted to where the Egyptian princess was bathing. She was also the one who offered to find an Israelite woman to care for the boy until he was old enough to go and live with his adopted mother in the palace of Pharaoh. In the genealogy of the Israelites, only Moses, Aaron, and Miriam are listed as children of their parents. It is possible that they had another sibling, but it is probable that Miriam was the one who provided for Moses to be saved from the water and have an Egyptian princess as his adopted mother.

After the Israelites were freed from Pharaoh, and in the moments after the drowning of the Egyptians at the Sea of Reeds, Moses sings a song of triumph. Just after Moses' song, Miriam leads all the women of the camp in the same two lines that Moses sang in the beginning of his song. She also leads them in the playing of the tambourine and in dancing. Scholars think that Miriam's song may be some of the oldest words in the entire scripture, used to begin Moses' song, but perhaps also part of a ritual to commemorate the crossing of the Sea of Reeds for centuries before the story was even written down.

Finally, there is a story about Miriam and Aaron being very human. Moses has received all the credit and praise during the Exodus, and he hasn't even followed his own rules. Moses apparently broke a rule about marrying someone outside the Israelite group, a Cushite. Aaron and Miriam bring this up and then ask why he seems to suggest to the people that he is the only one who speaks for God. Aaron and Miriam are considered prophets, too. Miriam was, after all, Moses' big sister, so, even taking into consideration the role of women in this period, being ignored by Moses and completely eclipsed by him must have been frustrating. God calls them all together and chastises Miriam and Aaron, striking only Miriam with leprosy. Miriam may be a prophet, but Moses is the only one God says God speaks to face to face (in Hebrew, literally "mouth to mouth").

Although Miriam learns that she is not in the same league with Moses, she continues to be revered as a prophet of Israel. In Numbers 20:1, the Israelites record her death and burial, something that is significant, because of the great status she, Aaron, and Moses have in the community.

It is hard to over-emphasize the importance of Miriam's role in Israel's journey to Canaan, first by her role in Moses' life when he was growing up, and then later as a prophet for the people. Although references to her are few, the references that we do have are significant because it would take a pretty important woman to be mentioned alongside such powerful figures as Moses and Aaron. God worked through Miriam to save the people—perhaps not in the same way God worked through Moses, but it was most definitely evident.

Theological Underpinnings
Often in the lives of characters in scripture, we see people who want to be at the very top. When they get there, they can become guilty of abusing their power. Moses was the one through whom God chose to free the Israelites. Miriam also was used by God for the same purpose. Just because her role wasn't spotlighted, she cannot be forgotten, and she must be revered in our study of the text.

We can think of other characters in scripture who weren't the most important in the eyes of the scripture writers, but whose roles were nevertheless very important. Joseph's brothers did not have the prominence of Joseph, but they became the ancestors of the twelve tribes of Israel. John the Baptist was not the Messiah, but the role he played in revealing Christ to the world was very important.

Since most people will not be the first or at the top, we need to be sure that the roles of the supporting characters in scripture are remembered and revered. When we have the opportunity to live lives that point to someone else (as Christians, all we do should point to Christ), we hopefully will not feel inferior, but realize that even our roles are important for God's purposes.

Notes:

Notes:

Applying the Lesson to Your Own Life

Think about a time that you have worked in, or walked in, the shadow of someone else. Sometimes that may have been comfortable and easy. You may have helped them get their start or helped to celebrate a great accomplishment.

Maybe there was a time when you wanted some of the glory for yourself, too. That is a very understandable human emotion. It can be easy to become jealous, especially when the person who is above us makes a mistake or does not live up to their own rules for others.

We may all want to be Moses, but when we find ourselves in the role of Miriam, we should remember how important that role is.

The Lesson

Get Started (12 min.)

Option 1: Call to Worship

Begin with Tambourines and dancing!

Turn to Exodus 15:20, and compose a melody to go with the scripture: (alternatively you may chant together)
"Sing to the LORD, for God has triumphed gloriously! Horse and rider God has thrown into the sea!"

Let the kids know that this is a celebration; they don't have to have perfect pitch to sing to God!

Leader Tip:
This may be a good opportunity to use something from your lesson in worship. Perhaps your song could be used as a call to worship while people play instruments and dance in the sanctuary.

Discussion Questions:
- What must it have been like for the Israelites to see the way God had answered their cries and taken away their pursuers?
- When have you been excited enough about something that all you could do is shout and sing and dance?
- If you haven't ever felt that way, what kind of circumstance could you imagine that might make you feel that way?

Pray: *Lord, God, you have shown yourself to be faithful in our scripture. When people were in need, you were always there. Come among us during this lesson. Be with us, and help us to know what you want us to learn from the example of your servant Miriam. Remind us that however we are called to serve you in our lives, it is important that we do our best to follow and be obedient to your will. Amen.*

Option 2: Call to Wake Up

Ask for volunteers for a pantomime. A pantomime is a way of expressing information or telling a story without words. This can be done by using body movements and facial expressions to act out a story or idea to an audience.

Have a mother and father, a baby Moses, a Miriam, and an Egyptian princess. Have the volunteers read the story in Exodus 2— about Moses' birth, about how he was found by the Egyptian princess, and how his own mother ended up caring for him for the Egyptian princess. Have the volunteers act out the scene in pantomime (no words!), and then ask the rest of the group to explain what happened in the story.

Discussion Questions:
- How do you think the Israelite parents felt when they were told that if they had male children, they were supposed to be killed as soon as they were delivered?
- How do you think Moses' parents felt when they chose to send Moses in a basket in the river? What would have made it so hard?
- How do you think Moses' sister, Miriam, felt?
- What would you have done if you were Miriam?
- How do you think Miriam felt, knowing that Moses was being raised in the Egyptian palace while she and the rest of the Hebrews were slaves to the Egyptians?

Notes:

Notes:

 # Listen Up (15 min.)

Say: *Miriam is a hero of the Old Testament story of the Exodus, the story of the Israelite people being saved by God through Moses, freed from Egyptian slavery, and led to the promised land of Canaan. Miriam was Moses' sister. When Moses was born, the Egyptians were afraid of the Israelite people because they were becoming too numerous. The Pharaoh decided to kill all the male children of the Israelites so they would not have so many people (capable fighting men) and threaten the Egyptian way of life: Egyptians in charge and Israelites as slaves.*

When Moses was born, his mother couldn't bear the thought of Moses being killed. So she hid him from the Egyptians for as long as she could. Eventually she was no longer able to hide Moses away, so instead of allowing him to be killed, she placed him in a basket and floated him on the Nile River. It is likely she chose the place to put him on the water because she knew Pharaoh's daughter would likely be bathing there. She set Moses up for success by having his sister Miriam watch after him to see what would happen. When the princess found Moses, she couldn't bear to see him killed either. Seeing that the princess wanted to care for the boy, Miriam approached the princess, probably not a safe thing to do, and offered to find an Israelite mother to care for him until he was old enough to live in the palace with the princess. Miriam arranged for Moses' own mother (and Miriam's mother) to care for Moses until he went to live with Pharaoh.

Discussion Questions:
- What do observe about the way Miriam cared for her brother?
- How would you have felt if you sent your brother to live in a palace while you had to remain as a slave?

Say: *When Moses left, Miriam stayed behind. She didn't know that Moses was set apart to be the one to deliver the Israelites. But she was a slave while he grew up as the son of a princess. When Moses killed an Egyptian and had to leave Egypt, Miriam stayed a slave in Egypt, as she had always been. When Moses came back to free the Israelites, Miriam was still a slave. When the Israelites finally gained freedom, Miriam was considered to be a prophet along with Moses and Aaron (Moses' brother who spoke on his behalf).*

Miriam led the women in singing and dancing just after Pharaoh's army was killed in the sea.

Discussion Questions:
- What kind of a person leads singing and dancing in front of people?
- Do you think you could be that kind of person? Why or why not?

Say: *She shared leadership with Moses and Aaron, but even that seems to have been difficult for her. When Moses married a Cushite woman (an action that broke his own rule of marrying those outside the Israelite people), Miriam and Aaron became angry. They started by criticizing Moses' choice of wife (this is a different story than the one in which Moses married a Midianite woman in the wilderness) and then they let loose an anger they had probably had for a long time. Why does everyone think God only talks to you Moses? We are prophets, too. We deserve credit.*

God called all three of them to the tent of meeting and spoke to them. While God confirmed Miriam as a prophet whom God spoke to in dreams and riddles, God said that Moses was a different kind of prophet. Many translations say God said God spoke to Moses "face to face." The Hebrew says God spoke to Moses "mouth to mouth." God had a different relationship with Moses than any prophet had previously had.

Essentially, God told Miriam and Aaron that even though they were prophets, they had no right to question Moses' authority. God caused Miriam to contract leprosy, and although Moses prayed for her to be cured and God did cure her, the whole company of Israelites had to wait seven days while Miriam spent her time outside the camp (she was unclean) before she could be let back in.

Discussion Questions:
- Have you ever been jealous of someone who had more authority than you? Would it be harder for you to follow if that person was your younger sibling?
- Do you think Aaron and Miriam had a legitimate point when they criticized Moses? Why or why not?
- Why do you think only Miriam was given a skin disease and not both Aaron and Miriam?

Notes:

Notes:

Now What? (20 min.)

Say: Many of us want to be leaders or the person in charge. Our tendency is to gravitate toward the starring roles, but most likely, we will find ourselves in supporting roles at some point in our life. In other words, when there is someone who receives great accolades because of a starring role they have, there is almost always a large group of people who helped them to get to that point. Maybe in the school play there is one star, but several supporting actors, people who design and move scenery, and also people who work the lighting and the sound. Without them the play could never happen. Or in sports, there is only one star quarterback, but there are several players who defend the line of scrimmage so the quarterback can excel.

Sometimes those who are behind the scenes do not receive enough credit for the parts that they play in life. Miriam is one of these characters. She saved Moses' life and arranged for him to be raised and taken care of in the palace of the Pharaoh. Moses sang and celebrated the victory over the Egyptians, but Miriam also sang. Scholars think Miriam's song is probably even older in the tradition of scripture than Moses' song. That means that it was likely sung as a remembrance of the victory for many years before the scripture was written down, and Moses' song was probably written or reconstructed using Miriam's song as a guide.

When Miriam saw inconsistency in Moses, she was willing to speak out, and likely her pride got the better of her. But her words about Moses breaking his own rules were important to point out. Even though she paid for her pride in her confrontation with Moses, she was still greatly revered by the Israelites as a prophet, and her death and burial are recorded in scripture in the way people of great honor are remembered.

Discussion Questions:
- Have you ever felt that your contributions were overlooked or that you were secondary to someone else? How did you react in that situation?
- When someone else has the greatest attention, is that frustrating to you? Is it maybe more comfortable for you?
- Do you think our modern society gives enough credit to those who aren't the "stars" in whatever field they are

in? Is it sometimes hard to be in the background and feel appreciated?
- Who do you look to for your worth or value? Where do you search for acceptance or approval?

It takes people in many different roles to make things work properly. Without Miriam, Moses would not have been where he was, and the Israelite people might not have been saved through him. (God would surely have found a way, but the way God chose used Miriam).

Discussion Question:
- How can we honor ourselves when we are in supporting roles? How can we value others?

Live It (5 min.)

Say: *As we leave this lesson, think about those in your life who may be in supporting roles to the things you do. Maybe this would be your parents, your siblings, your friends, your teachers, or many others in your life. What can you do to make sure those people know that you appreciate what they have done in your life? How can you thank them?*

End with prayer:
Gracious God, you call people into your service in so many ways. Sometimes we may find ourselves in the position of Moses, the center of attention. When we do, help us to fulfill your call faithfully, and help us to give credit to all those who help us to be and do all the things we are able to be and do. More likely, we will find ourselves in the role of Miriam, supporting someone who is doing things in the spotlight while we are helping. When we are in these roles, remind us that the things we are doing are important and are your special call in our lives. Help us to complete whatever task you give to us, whether it seems big or small, with the same joy and faithfulness. Help us to work for your glory, not for praise and recognition of our own efforts, knowing that our worth and value is found in Christ alone.

Just In Case:

Where did Miriam Dance?

The book of Exodus most often has a translation of the place where the Egyptians were killed as "the Red Sea." This is not what the Hebrew actually states. The place where the Israelites crossed-over on dry land and the Egyptians were killed, is the Hebrew phrase, "yam suf," or Sea of Reeds. According to Bernard F. Botto, the sea of Reeds was likely thought of by the Israelites as "the sea at the end of the earth." The Red Sea is a specific location, but it is uncertain whether that is the same as the "yam suf," or if the sea of Reeds was in another location entirely.

Just In Case:

Should Miriam have Danced?

Rabbis over the centuries have used a form known as the "Midrash" to expound upon and explain the scriptures found in their ancient texts to followers of Judaism. One Midrash explanation states that when the Egyptians were drowning in the sea of Reeds, the angels in heaven wanted to celebrate the victory won for the Israelites. Instead, God asked them how they could celebrate while God's children were perishing.

We must always be certain to remember that all people are God's children, made in God's image, and whenever any of God's children suffer, God mourns.

In Christ's name,
Amen

Resources used:
New Interpreter's Study Bible, Abingdon Press, Nashville, TN, 2003; A Journey Through the Hebrew Scriptures, Frances S. Frick, Wadsworth, Toronto, ONT, 2003; The New Interpreter's Bible: A Commentary in Twelve Volumes, Abingdon Press, Nashville, TN, 1998; http://rorycooney.blogspot.com/2013/03/my-creations-are-drowning-and-you-are.html

© 2014 Discipleship Ministry Team of the Ministry Council of the Cumberland Presbyterian Church. All Rights Reserved.

Miriam's Life

Three major moments in Miriam's life are outlined in this lesson.

1. Miriam was almost certainly the sister of Moses who stood by as Moses floated down the river to the place where the Pharaoh's daughter was bathing. Miriam made sure Moses was safe, and she arranged for their mother to take care of Moses until he was old enough to live with his adopted mother in the palace.

2. Miriam led all the women of the Israelites in singing, dancing, and playing the tambourine in celebration of the victory over the Egyptians.

3. Miriam complained against Moses, and, although she kind of had a point, God disciplined her for speaking against Moses.

In which of these major moments in Miriam's life is it easiest to see myself? Would I do the same thing in her situation?

Which of these moments seems the most unlikely in my life? How would I react in her situation?

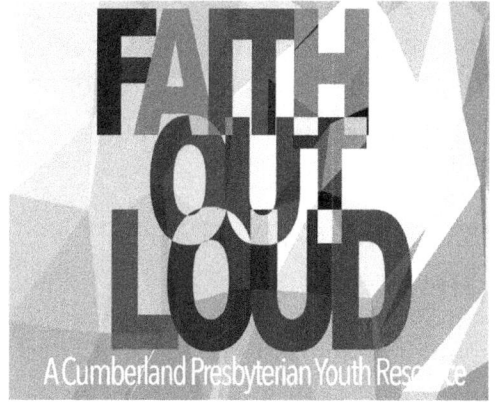

Jephthah's Daughter:
Our Words Have Consequences!
by Melissa Reid Goodloe

Scripture: Judges 11:30-39

Theme: When we commit to doing something for God or others, we should follow through no matter the consequences. Sometimes it is necessary to follow through with what is right, even when others speak too quickly.

Resource List

- Bowl
- Water
- Stones (Small river rocks or decorative stones about the size of a half dollar)
- Handout –"Jephthah's Daughter"
- Pens/pencils

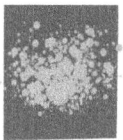

Leader Prep

- Collect stones or river rocks prior to class.
- Copy the handout "Jephthah's Daughter" for each student.

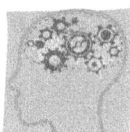

Leader Insight

Connecting to Your Students
Many young people have experienced their share of broken promises; they've broken promises and had others break promises. Trust is easily broken. It can be hard to focus on keeping our word, instead of reliving a broken promise.

Most students will not remember a time when a person's word and a handshake was all that was needed to make a binding promise. Today, contracts and witnesses, or the threat of lawsuit to uphold a promise, are needed to keep a promise. This lesson will explore a tough decision to keep a commitment to God, even when it cost a life.

Explaining the Bible
The book of Judges records Jephthah as a judge over Israel for a period of six years (Judges 12:7). He lived in Gilead

Notes:

and was a member of the tribe of Manasseh. His father's name is also given as Gilead, and his mother is described as a prostitute; this could mean that his father might have been any of the men from Gilead.

The Israelites "again did what was evil in the sight of the Lord...they forsook the Lord and did not serve him. So the anger of the Lord was kindled against Israel, and he sold them into the hand of the Philistines and into the hand of the Ammonites..." (Judges 10:6-7).

Jephthah listened to God's instructions, and God delivered him and his army in many battles.

The elders of Gilead ask him to be their leader in the campaign against the Ammonites, but he held out for a more permanent and prominent position. The elders agree that, provided Jephthah succeeds in defeating Ammon, he will be their permanent chieftain. On behalf of Israel as a whole, and in reliance on the might of God the Judge, Jephthah challenged the Ammonites.

Jephthah wanted to offer something pleasing to God as a sacrifice for his good fortune.

Jephthah made the oath, "whatever comes out of the door of my house to meet me when I return in triumph from the Ammonites will be the Lord's, and I will sacrifice it as a burnt offering." (Judges 11:31)

The victorious Jephthah is met on his return by his daughter, his only child. You can imagine how his rash vow pounded in his mind as she ran out to greet him.

Jephthah tears his clothes and cries, "Alas, my daughter! You have brought me very low!" But Jephthah is bound by his vow: "I have opened my mouth to the Lord, and I cannot take back my vow." (Judges 11:35)

Jephthah's daughter showed strength and courage in the face of death. She stated that an oath made to the Lord must be kept. Her only request was two month to mourn her virginity. And then Jephthah "did with her according to his vow that he had made." (Judges 11:39)

Jephthah's daughter was a woman of character. The Bible does not mention her by name but does reference her being honored years after her death.

God wants our commitment. We need to follow God's will, but should not make promises based on need or crisis. We need to be able to fulfill our promises to God.

Theological Underpinnings
Jephthah spoke without thinking first. It was tradition for the ladies of the village to greet the heroes as they returned from war. Since he had no wife, Jephthah should have known his only daughter would be leading the processional to greet him.

High value was placed on marriage and motherhood among women. Jephthah's daughter realized she would never have either of these rites of passage.

There is a debate among scholars as to whether Jephthah's daughter was actually killed. Human ritual killings were frowned upon. Most biblical scholars take the Bible to mean she was literally killed. However, there are some Rabbis who believe she was given to God in the form of a living sacrifice. She would have spent the rest of her days in service to the church. This was why she mourned her virginity because she would never marry or have children.

Applying the Lesson to Your Own Life
Have you ever spoken before you thought? Have you ever promised something without thinking?

If so, it probably didn't result in the death of someone. Even so, our words mean something. Our promises mean something. Our promises to God mean everything. Are you someone who keeps your word, or do you make so many promises, it's hard to keep them all straight?

Would it be better to follow through with a bad idea or break a promise?

How can you keep from making promises you cannot keep?

Notes:

Notes:

The Lesson

Get Started (10 min.)

Post signs in the four corners of the room: Strongly Agree, Agree, Disagree, Strongly Disagree.

Read each statement and decide how you feel about it. The students should move to the corner of the room that coincides with how they feel about the question.

1. Someone who breaks a promise is not trustworthy.

Strongly Agree   Agree   Disagree   Strongly Disagree

2. Breaking a promise is okay once in a while.

Strongly Agree   Agree   Disagree   Strongly Disagree

3. If someone breaks a promise, it means he or she didn't really mean it.

Strongly Agree   Agree   Disagree   Strongly Disagree

4. A reputation is built on how one keeps or breaks promises.

Strongly Agree   Agree   Disagree   Strongly Disagree

After a minute of discussion for each question, have a representative from each corner report a summary of their discussion. (Example: We strongly disagree that it is okay to break a promise because trust is fragile, and breaking a promise will cause friends to lose faith in you.)

Gather the group back together.

Ask students to think of a promise they made recently. While students think of a recent promise, set out the bowl of water.

Give each student a stone. Ask them to drop the stone into the bowl of water, one at a time. Ask each person to count the ripples their stone makes. Remembering that number, ask them to write down the names (ripples) of people affected by that promise.

Discussion Questions:
- Now imagine you promised to sacrifice the first person listed. How would you feel?
- If you knew that your promise was life or death for the people around you, would you have made it so quickly?

Listen Up (20 min.)

Have someone read Judges 11:30-39. (If more background is needed, have the group read the entire 11th chapter of Judges.)

Pass out the handout titled, "Jephthah's Daughter." Divide your group into small groups to discuss. After initial discussion in the small groups, pull the larger group together and share answers.

Discussion Questions:
- What oath did Jephthah make?
- Did you think something bad might happen? What made you think that?
- Who met Jephthah when he returned?
- How did Jephthah react?
- How did his daughter respond to his hasty promise? What did you think about the way Jephthah's daughter responded to her father's vow?
- How would you have responded if you had been Jephthah's child?

Say: *Promises do not affect just one person. There is a ripple effect.*

Notes:

Notes:

Now What? (15 min.)

Gather the group back together.

Discussion Questions:
- How have you felt in the following situations?
  - When you have made a promise under stressful circumstances
  - When you have broken a promise to someone you cared about
  - When you had a promise made to you and then broken about something that was really important

God wants our promises and faithfulness in helping others, loving our neighbor, etc.
- What are some examples of poor promises?
- What promises can you make to God and keep?

Live It (5 min.)

Ask for prayer requests, and close with the following prayer: *Dear God, Help me to think before I speak. I wish to follow your will and make only promises that will glorify you. Amen*

Resources used:
Betsy Flikkemar, Learning to Give

© 2014 Discipleship Ministry Team of the Ministry Council of the Cumberland Presbyterian Church. All Rights Reserved.

Jephthah's Daughter

What oath did Jephthah make?

Who met Jephthah when he returned?

How did Jephthah react?

How did his daughter respond to his hasty promise?

How would you have responded if you had been Jephthah's child?

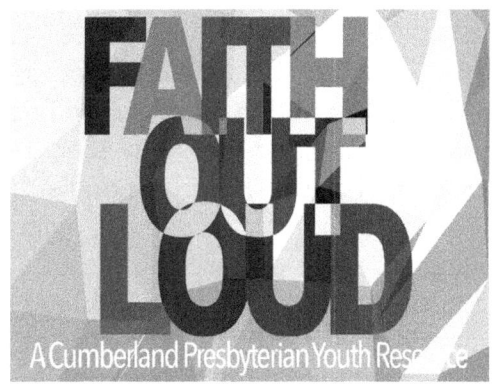

Dorcas / Tabitha
by Andy McClung

Scripture: Acts 9:36-43, James 2:20,26, Matthew 25:34-45, Isaiah 6:8

Theme: Christians do good works as a grateful response to God.

Resource List

- Printer paper
- Pens, one per student
- A green marker or crayon
- $1 or $5 bill to use as a prize
- (Optional) Recording of the Matthew West song, "Do Something."
- (Optional) Video capability (laptop, projector, DVD player, speakers, etc.)

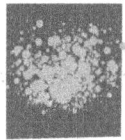

Leader Prep

- Make photocopies of the handout "Called to Serve," found at the end of the lesson. Separate each story or scripture.

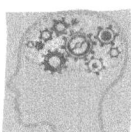

Leader Insight

Connecting to Your Students
Your students may not be familiar with the movie Clueless (1995), but they may be much like its main character: a rich, self-absorbed teen who does good things because it's trendy, and it makes her feel good. She's clueless about how real people -- not rich, not beautiful, not popular -- live, think, and feel. Working at a canned food drive and giving out unsolicited fashion advice are equally good actions to her. Her good works are born from pity and pride rather than any sense of morality.

Nowadays, it's trendy to be environmentally aware, socially active, etc., but teens who do these things may be doing them quite possibly out of something other than theological conviction. They may simply be going along with the trend. Worse, they may think that being aware of needs and talking about doing good things is equivalent to actually doing good things.

Notes:

Explaining the Bible

When we read Acts 9:36-43, we may be tempted to focus on the obvious miracle: Simon Peter bringing a woman back from death. That's a reasonable thing to focus on. After all, the book is "The Acts of the Apostles," and Simon Peter is an apostle. Plus, raising someone from death is quite an attention-grabber. Since this series of lessons is about women, though, let's focus not on Simon Peter but instead on the woman he raised from death. The obvious lesson to draw from her story is that death is not the end for those who have entrusted their lives to Christ. It's easy to parallel her story of being raised from death back to life with our hope of being resurrected after death to live eternally. But for the purpose of this lesson, let's look beyond the obvious.

The first thing we may notice about the woman in this story is that she is called by two names: Dorcas and Tabitha. This is the first time in the New Testament that this is done for a woman. Luke, who wrote Acts, may have included both versions of her name because she was known by both names. Joppa, a major Mediterranean seaport, was quite multi-cultural. Maybe Dorcas/Tabitha's ministry was to Jews and Gentiles alike, and Luke wanted to ensure that everyone who read his book and had heard of her good works realized that Tabitha and Dorcas were the same woman. Remember, in Acts the Church is growing from being a subset of Judaism into a multi-cultural organization, so this is not a far-fetched idea.

It is important to notice that Dorcas/Tabitha is called "a disciple" in verse 36. That means she was a follower of the Way of Christ. She wasn't just a good person. She wasn't just a nice person. She was a person who did good things because she knew and followed Christ.

So what was it that Dorcas/Tabitha did that was so good? "She was devoted to good works and acts of charity" (Acts 9:36 NRSV). In verse 39, we learn that at least one of these good works was making clothes for widows. We don't know if she bought the fabric and sewed clothes, if she wove the fabric herself, or if she gathered scraps of fabric that washed ashore in Joppa's harbor. We don't know if she also made clothes for poor men and children. We don't know if she was rich or poor, old or young. What we do know is that in the ancient world a woman with no husband to provide for her had very few opportunities to earn a living on her own. She had to rely on charity to survive. Thus, widows were at the bottom of the economic ladder. Sadly, the same is still true in many countries today.

In that culture, a husband provided for his wife. After he died the oldest son took care of her. If he died the next oldest son would take care of her. There is no mention of Tabitha's family in Acts, so she may have been a sonless widow herself. If so, she turned cultural expectations upside down. According to cultural expectations, she was supposed to be a burden on others, but she became a benefactor to others. This was just as surprising and backwards as a dead woman being raised to life again.

Acts of charity, or doing good works, have always been a part of living life as a disciple of Jesus Christ. Since at least 1834, Christians in certain areas, inspired by Dorcas/Tabitha, have come together to form Dorcas Societies. These organizations do works of charity. The first Dorcas Societies focused on making and distributing plain, basic articles of clothing to those in need. Later, some societies branched out and offered other services as well.

Dorcas/Tabitha did plenty to spread the love of Christ on her own, but what God did for her, through Peter, spread the gospel even more effectively. When the people of Joppa heard that she had been raised from death, many of them came to believe in Jesus.

Theological Underpinnings
Cumberland Presbyterians believe in doing good things. Cumberland Presbyterians do good works. Our Confession of Faith says that one thing we do in worship -- in addition to giving God praise, thanksgiving, love, and confessing our sins -- is commit to serve (5.13). The church as a whole "never exists for [itself] alone" (5.09). In other words, a congregation that is only taking care of its members isn't fully being the church. Likewise, a Christian who isn't doing acts of service isn't fully being a Christian. But one important thing to keep in mind is that we don't do good things in order to be saved through Christ; we do good things because we are saved through Christ. The Confession puts it this way: "Good works are the result of, and not the means of, salvation (6.08). Furthermore, our Confession really emphasizes that all the good things we do are done in grateful response to what God has done for us.

We glorify God, not ourselves, by doing good works. These good works include acts of service and mercy that we know Jesus did, as well as making Christ-like ethical and moral

Notes:

Notes:

choices in our relationships with other people, our own bodies, with money, and with creation (6.09). Some of these good works can, and should, be helping those in need, like Tabitha did.

Looking at Church history beyond our own denomination, it's clear that the Church was never intended to be a place where members simply gave money to support professional ministers, but rather a place where all members pooled their abilities, gifts, and resources to do ministry together.

Applying the Lesson to Your Own Life
What "good works and acts of charity" do you do on a regular basis? Are there other good works you feel called to do, but don't? If so, what's stopping you?

List all of your abilities, skills, resources, connections, and gifts on a piece of paper. Beside each item, write three ways it could be used to serve those in need.

Does your congregation equip and encourage members to be engaged in meaningful ministry? Does your congregation create opportunities for doing so? If not, why not? Has the original purpose for the Church changed just for your congregation? If your congregation does equip and encourage members to do good works, are children and teens included with those who are called on to do ministry?

Who gets the glory for you and your congregation's good works, the worker(s) or God?

The Lesson

Get Started (15 min.)

Have students stand. Give each student a piece of paper.

Have a green marker or crayon available. If you have a really large class, have two or three markers.

Explain that you're going to make a human bar graph. Each student will be a bar on the graph, representing his or her answer to the same question.

Discussion Question:
- How much do you think it costs, on average, just to live one day in the United States?

Announce that the first student whose estimate matches the correct answer will win a prize: the one or five dollar bill.

Going in alphabetical order by middle name, have students, one-by-one, write their estimates on their papers in whole dollars (i.e. no cents). No two students may give the same answer. If someone tries, make them change their estimate by going at least one dollar higher or lower.

Now have students arrange themselves as if they are a bar graph: the lowest estimate on the left, the highest estimate on the right, and all others in proportionally ascending order in between. This would work best if students have their backs to a wall. Being a human graph may mean some students have to sit, squat, hunch, or hold their papers high above their heads. That's part of the fun. Be sure to take a photograph of the completed graph.

Announce that the actual average cost to live for one day in the United States is $55. Give the prize money to anyone with this exact estimate (or the closest estimate if no one guesses it correctly).

If you think it's necessary, explain that while we may not hand over $55 to someone each and every day, this number is derived from taking the average annual cost of food, clothes, housing, transportation, medical care, utilities, etc. and dividing it by 365.

Notes:

Notes:

Leader Tip:
If necessary, nudge students with some suggestions. "If someone has enough money to buy stuff to fix their house, but they're too old or sick or something to do the work… is that someone in need?" "If a single mother leaves her little kids at home by themselves a lot because she works two or three jobs… is she in need?"

If any students' estimates were vastly higher or lower than $55, ask them what they were basing their estimates on.

Discussion Question:
- What would be the worst thing about being really poor?

If any students claim to be poor, be understanding but say something like the following: If you have access to a car, if you have more clothes than the ones you're wearing, if you have eaten more than once in the last 30 hours, if you slept last night surrounded by four walls and roof, (look directly at the student who won the cash prize earlier) if you have cash in your pocket, then compared to many people in the world, you are rich.

Discussion Questions:
- How do you, personally, define "poor?"
- What situations, besides poverty, could cause someone to need help?

Transition to the lesson by saying something like: *In this world, there are always going to be people in need. Some of them are poor and need food, clothes, and shelter. Some are stranded or lost and need transportation. Some need help doing some particular project. There are a lot of ways people might be in need. And, there are lots of ways we can do good things to help people in need.*

Listen Up (15 min.)

Discussion Question:
- Does anyone know what your name means?

Allow any students who know it to share the meaning of their names.

Ask each student who answered:
- Do you think your name accurately reflects who you are?

Briefly allow answers.

What would you expect a person named Dorcas to be like? Briefly allow answers. Don't scold anyone for offering a negative or unflattering response. It is a pretty dorky-sounding name in English.

Say: *Let's see if you're right.*

Have someone read aloud Acts 9:36-43.

Explain that "Tabitha" is the Aramaic word for "gazelle" and "Dorcas" is the Greek word for "gazelle." So this dorky-sounding Greek name really reflects a beautiful and graceful creature. (Aramaic is a sister language to Hebrew and is what Jesus and Galileans spoke in everyday life, even though they likely also knew Hebrew.)

Say: *Back then, women were more likely than men to be poor. Why do you think that was?*

Say: *Today in the United States 56% of poor people are women compared with 44% who are men. Worldwide, 60% of poor people are women.*

Discussion Question:
- Why do you think there are more poor women than men?

Using the background material, explain the plight of widows in the ancient world.

- Why do you think all those widows were so upset at Tabitha's death?
- Why do you think Tabitha decided to make clothes for poor widows?

If a student doesn't bring it up, point out that making clothes is what she knew how to do. If she'd been a baker, she probably would have given out bread to the hungry. If she'd been a carpenter, she probably would have built stuff for the needy. If she'd been a fisherman, she probably would have given away fish. But she could make clothes, so she did. She used the abilities she had to serve others.

Say: *God doesn't normally call us to become something we're not in order to serve others. God doesn't normally miraculously make us able to do things beyond our abilities so*

Notes:

Leader Tip:
You may wish to point out that widows would often go to the home of a recently deceased person as public mourners, a way to announce the death to the community regardless of whether the widows knew the deceased or not. These widows, however, seem to have known Dorcas/Tabitha and benefited from her good works.

Notes:

that we can serve those in need. God calls us, as we are, to use what we already have to serve.

Give the students pens or pencils and, on the backs of the papers they used in the opening exercise, have them make a list of every ability, skill, resource, connection, and gift they have.

After they are finished, have the students write next to their items three ways that skill, ability, resource, etc., could be used to serve those in need.

Then name each student, one–by-one, and have the rest of the class identify a skill, ability, resource, etc. they recognize in that student which they think can be used to serve those in need. If the student in focus has written down that skill, ability, resource, etc. on his or her own list, he or she should circle it. Try to keep the length of time equal for each student. Also, try to have at least one such thing to say about each student yourself, just in case the other students don't. If you have visitors whom no one knows just say, "Since we're just getting to know you, why don't you share one of the things you wrote about yourself?"

Now What? (15 min.)

Distribute the "Called to Serve" handout found at the end of the lesson, which you have already cut and separated. Have a different student read each part in the order they are listed. Include about twenty seconds of silence after each reading.

#1 Leo
Leo is a Cumberland Presbyterian minister who, instead of serving a congregation, felt called to minister to people experiencing homelessness. To better understand what it's like to be homeless, Leo spent several months living as a homeless person. With the knowledge and experience he gained, he started two ministries for homeless people in Memphis. One ministry, located in a local church's building, provides a hot

meal, overnight shelter in a safe place, a warm bed, and a hot shower to twelve homeless persons one night a week during the winter months. The other ministry organizes volunteers to make and distribute burritos to homeless persons one night a week. Leo had no money of his own to get these ministries started, but that didn't stop him. He used his connections with the right people to make it all happen.

#2 Matthew 25:34-45 (NLT)
"Then the King will say to those on his right, 'Come, you who are blessed by my Father, inherit the Kingdom prepared for you from the creation of the world. For I was hungry, and you fed me. I was thirsty, and you gave me a drink. I was a stranger, and you invited me into your home. I was naked, and you gave me clothing. I was sick, and you cared for me. I was in prison, and you visited me.'
"Then these righteous ones will reply, 'Lord, when did we ever see you hungry and feed you? Or thirsty and give you something to drink? Or a stranger and show you hospitality? Or naked and give you clothing? When did we ever see you sick or in prison and visit you?'
"And the King will say, 'I tell you the truth, when you did it to one of the least of these my brothers and sisters, you were doing it to me!'
"Then the King will turn to those on the left and say, 'Away with you, you cursed ones, into the eternal fire prepared for the devil and his demons. For I was hungry, and you didn't feed me. I was thirsty, and you didn't give me a drink. I was a stranger, and you didn't invite me into your home. I was naked, and you didn't give me clothing. I was sick and in prison, and you didn't visit me.'
"Then they will reply, 'Lord, when did we ever see you hungry or thirsty or a stranger or naked or sick or in prison, and not help you?'
"And he will answer, 'I tell you the truth, when you refused to help the least of these my brothers and sisters, you were refusing to help me.'"

#3 Peggy
Peggy was connected with a Cumberland Presbyterian church in Chattanooga. She was also a nurse in the neonatal intensive care unit at a local hospital, where newborn babies with serious health issues are taken. Many of Peggy's patients were prematurely-born babies. She noticed that the parents of most of these premature babies had enough clothes and diapers for full-term babies, but the premature births had caught them by surprise and they didn't have anything that would fit their extra-tiny newborns. So Peggy started making

Notes:

Notes:

extra-small outfits to give to these parents. From then on, every premature baby got a beautiful, hand-made outfit from her, which gave those distressed parents one less thing to worry about during a frightening and heart-wrenching time.

#4 Isaiah 6:8 (NLT)
Then I heard the Lord asking, "Whom should I send as a messenger to this people? Who will go for us?"
I said, "Here I am. Send me."

#5 Ollie
Ollie is a Cumberland Presbyterian elder who worked all his life running a restaurant in Birmingham. He regularly and generously gave money to various ministries over the years, but running a restaurant takes a lot of time, so Ollie just didn't have much time to give… until he retired in his 60s. In retirement, Ollie started going on, and eventually organizing, short-term mission trips to repair and rebuild houses damaged or destroyed by hurricanes and tornadoes. He has also gone to Colombia, South America a few times to help build a retirement home for senior citizens and to do repairs on a school for children. He was never trained in construction, but learned how to do these things in order to serve others.

#6 James 2:20, 26 (NLT)
Can't you see that faith without good deeds is useless? Just as the body is dead without breath, so also faith is dead without good works.

#7 Kristi and Eric
Kristi and Eric, a Cumberland Presbyterian married couple, left their jobs and their home in Tennessee to move to Illinois, more than 300 miles and five hours away. They made this move so they could adopt three children and live in a community specifically designed to bring together retirees, children living in the foster care system, and adoptive parents. In this community, neglected, abused, and abandoned children who previously felt as if no one wanted them, gain parents, grandparents, and siblings. Retired adults, who often lose their sense of purpose in life, find a new purpose in offering these children and their adoptive parents support, wisdom, and help.

#8 Acts 9:36 (NLT)
There was a believer in Joppa named Tabitha (which in Greek is Dorcas). She was always doing kind things for others and helping the poor.

Live It (5 min.)

Explain that you are going to offer up a question. Each student is to ask himself or herself the same question, and seek an answer during two full minutes of silent meditation.

When you're sure everyone understands and is ready to be still and silent, say: Ask yourself: "Like Tabitha, what good things can I do for others that will glorify God and help those in need?"

Maintain two minutes of silence.

If you have the ability to show YouTube videos in class, show the one entitled Matthew West, "Do Something," posted by MatthewWestVEVO. Another option would be "Here I am Lord," by Dan Schutte, which could be sung a cappella or with a live musician. If you have no way of working either of these songs into the lesson, dismiss the class after the silence.

Resources used: Acts, by William Willimon. All the Women of the Bible, by Edith Deen. All the Women of the Bible, by Herbert Lockyer. isle-of-man.com. kff.org. opensourceecology.org. ucdavis.edu. undp.org.

© 2014 Discipleship Ministry Team of the Ministry Council of the Cumberland Presbyterian Church. All Rights Reserved.

Notes:

Called to Serve

#1 Leo
Leo is a Cumberland Presbyterian minister who, instead of serving a congregation, felt called to minister to people experiencing homelessness. To better understand what it's like to be homeless, Leo spent several months living as a homeless person. With the knowledge and experience he gained, he started two ministries for homeless people in Memphis. One ministry, located in a local church's building, provides a hot meal, overnight shelter in a safe place, a warm bed, and a hot shower to twelve homeless persons one night a week during the winter months. The other ministry organizes volunteers to make and distribute burritos to homeless persons one night a week. Leo had no money of his own to get these ministries started, but that didn't stop him. He used his connections with the right people to make it all happen.

#2 Matthew 25:34-45 (NLT)
"Then the King will say to those on his right, 'Come, you who are blessed by my Father, inherit the Kingdom prepared for you from the creation of the world. For I was hungry, and you fed me. I was thirsty, and you gave me a drink. I was a stranger, and you invited me into your home. I was naked, and you gave me clothing. I was sick, and you cared for me. I was in prison, and you visited me.'
"Then these righteous ones will reply, 'Lord, when did we ever see you hungry and feed you? Or thirsty and give you something to drink? Or a stranger and show you hospitality? Or naked and give you clothing? When did we ever see you sick or in prison and visit you?'
"And the King will say, 'I tell you the truth, when you did it to one of the least of these my brothers and sisters, you were doing it to me!'
"Then the King will turn to those on the left and say, 'Away with you, you cursed ones, into the eternal fire prepared for the devil and his demons. For I was hungry, and you didn't feed me. I was thirsty, and you didn't give me a drink. I was a stranger, and you didn't invite me into your home. I was naked, and you didn't give me clothing. I was sick and in prison, and you didn't visit me.'
"Then they will reply, 'Lord, when did we ever see you hungry or thirsty or a stranger or naked or sick or in prison, and not help you?'
"And he will answer, 'I tell you the truth, when you refused to help the least of these my brothers and sisters, you were refusing to help me.'"

#3 Peggy
Peggy was connected with a Cumberland Presbyterian church in Chattanooga. She was also a nurse in the neonatal intensive care unit at a local hospital, where newborn babies with serious health issues are taken. Many of Peggy's patients were prematurely-born babies. She noticed that the parents of most of these premature babies had enough clothes and diapers for full-term babies, but the premature births had caught them by surprise and they didn't have anything that would fit their extra-tiny newborns. So Peggy started making extra-small outfits to give to these parents. From then on, every premature baby got a beautiful, hand-made outfit from her, which gave those distressed parents one less thing to worry about during a frightening and heart-wrenching time.

Called to Serve

#4 Isaiah 6:8 (NLT)
Then I heard the Lord asking, "Whom should I send as a messenger to this people? Who will go for us?"
I said, "Here I am. Send me."

#5 Ollie
Ollie is a Cumberland Presbyterian elder who worked all his life running a restaurant in Birmingham. He regularly and generously gave money to various ministries over the years, but running a restaurant takes a lot of time, so Ollie just didn't have much time to give… until he retired in his 60s. In retirement, Ollie started going on, and eventually organizing, short-term mission trips to repair and rebuild houses damaged or destroyed by hurricanes and tornadoes. He has also gone to Colombia, South America a few times to help build a retirement home for senior citizens and to do repairs on a school for children. He was never trained in construction, but learned how to do these things in order to serve others.

#6 James 2:20, 26 (NLT)
Can't you see that faith without good deeds is useless? Just as the body is dead without breath, so also faith is dead without good works.

#7 Kristi and Eric
Kristi and Eric, a Cumberland Presbyterian married couple, left their jobs and their home in Tennessee to move to Illinois, more than 300 miles and five hours away. They made this move so they could adopt three children and live in a community specifically designed to bring together retirees, children living in the foster care system, and adoptive parents. In this community, neglected, abused, and abandoned children who previously felt as if no one wanted them, gain parents, grandparents, and siblings. Retired adults, who often lose their sense of purpose in life, find a new purpose in offering these children and their adoptive parents support, wisdom, and help.

#8 Acts 9:36 (NLT)
There was a believer in Joppa named Tabitha (which in Greek is Dorcas). She was always doing kind things for others and helping the poor.

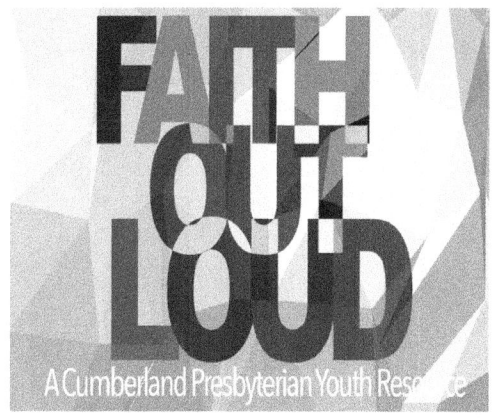

Hagar the Horrible?
by Chris Warren

Scripture: Genesis 16, 21:8-20

Theme: Although God fulfills the Covenant to Abraham by providing Isaac, through Sarah, God also makes a covenant with Hagar.

Resource List

- Chairs for Musical Chairs
- Music player (laptop, iPod, MP3 player, CD player, speakers, etc.)
- Picture of ancient temple in Jerusalem

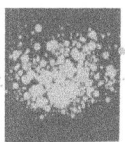

Leader Prep

- Arrange chairs for a game of musical chairs.
- Have music cued and ready to go for the game.
- Locate a picture of Jerusalem with the Dome of the Rock and the location of the Ancient Temple. The Internet is always a good place to look.

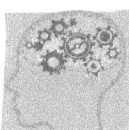

Leader Insight

Connecting to Your Students
While we may wish that the themes in this lesson were foreign to our students, they're most likely not. With themes like doubt about the way God answers our prayers, being forced into situations where we do not want to go, excitement about becoming elevated in the sight of those we admire (or at least those who have great authority), jealousy over a relationship that someone else has with a person we care about, and being cut off from people who are important to us, this is one intense story. Hopefully the youth we are teaching have not experienced many of these things, but the basic feelings of powerlessness, excitement, jealousy, and rejection are ones we can all relate to. Though this story has cultural references

> **Leader Tip:**
> I have chosen to use Abraham and Sarah instead of Abram and Sarai, even though in one portion of the story they are called by one set of names and later by the other. Hopefully using Abraham and Sarah throughout the lesson will reduce confusion.

that are unusual for us, the story, at its heart, is one we can easily relate to.

Explaining the Bible

God has promised Abraham a wonderful thing.

God has told Abraham that he will become the father of many nations. In the history of the Israelites, they would often speak of the origin of the 12 tribes— of Abraham becoming the father of Isaac, the grandfather of Jacob, and the 12 tribes of Israel being named after Jacob's sons. Not much attention is given to Abraham's other children, of which there are six. Abraham's first-born son, Ishmael, was the result of his union with Hagar, Sarah's Egyptian servant/slave. Isaac's second son belonged to Sarah, his wife.

Sarah was concerned because God had promised Abraham a son through whom these many nations would be born, but God had not yet allowed Sarah to have a child. Sarah arranged for Abraham to have a child with her servant because both Abraham and Sarah weren't getting any younger. This was a common practice, abhorrent to us, but it would not have been frowned upon in that culture.

Often Sarah is given a bad rap for not "trusting in God," but we have to remember that there is great scriptural evidence for people helping God's plans along. Often God works through the actions of people to accomplish God's purposes. So, perhaps it is unfair to chastise Sarah for her actions.

What is perhaps more disturbing about Sarah's actions is that, once the plan she has put together has been executed, and it works perfectly, she becomes jealous and treats her servant Hagar terribly. Even though Sarah was the one who suggested Abraham have a child with Hagar, Sarah grows bitterly jealous and takes it out on her. "But [Abraham] said to [Sarah], 'Your slave-girl is in your power; do to her as you please.' Then [Sarah] dealt harshly with her, and she ran away from her." (Genesis 16:6)

It is what happens once Hagar runs away that is the most wonderful part of the story for her, and most often missed by modern readers. God sends an angel to be with Hagar, and that angel gives almost exactly the same promise to Hagar that God had given to Abraham. Hagar is promised that her offspring will be so multiplied that they cannot be counted. Hagar becomes the only person in the Old Testament to give God a name (Elroi, or "the God who sees me"), and even though Abraham is the father, the name for the child is given through Hagar by the angel of the Lord.

Hagar is a heroine for her willingness to obey God, and because she herself sees God and becomes the mother of a great multitude through her son Ishmael. It is interesting that God gives such a similar promise to Hagar as the promise given to Abraham. God does not give such a promise to Sarah, but often we read the fulfillment of God's promise to Abraham as having come solely through Isaac. We also see God's care and mercy for those who are cast out of their communities.

Abraham is curiously silent in so much of this story. He quietly agrees to have a child with Hagar (Sarah's idea). When there is dissension between Sarah and Hagar, who in conceiving a child has now been raised to the status of a second wife, Abraham does nothing to ease the tension. Instead he lets Sarah deal with it however she wants to. Finally, when Hagar and Ishmael are sent away, it is because of Sarah's discomfort and complaints. Abraham's feelings are not discussed.

Theological Underpinnings

There are some extremely significant theological questions here. Who are the children of Abraham? To whom is the promise of God's covenant extended? In our modern world these questions are complicated by the idea that Jewish believers, and by extension Christian believers, trace their ancestry as the children of God through Abraham's son, Isaac, but Muslim believers trace their ancestry through Abraham's son, Ishmael. Often ignored are the five other sons of Abraham who were born to him after his wife Sarah died and he re-married. By the way, he must have been really old when these five were born.

At issue are God's promises and how they should be understood. Are God's promises available to all people, or are they only available through a certain ancestor. While scripture gives greater time and attention to the line of Isaac, the promises given to Hagar as Ishmael's mother are not only present in our scripture, but they are unique in scripture to be given to a woman. The promises Hagar receives have some similarities to the ones given to Mary when she conceives Jesus. As faithful students of scripture, we need to give Hagar her due and, by extension, Ishmael, because they, too, received the promises given to Abraham for his offspring. Through Hagar, God fulfilled God's promise. God fulfilled it again in Isaac.

Notes:

At issue also are the rights of women in this society. Things happen in this story that we can scarcely imagine in our day. These are things that should never have happened in any time, but they are told to us as a matter of fact because of the culture of the time of Hagar. This may bring up questions and concerns in your group. Theologically speaking, God does not want anyone to be in such a subservient relationship to another in any time, or for any person to mistreat someone because of jealousy. However, God was able to use even a horrible social structure to bring about good and fulfill God's promises. That doesn't make it OK, but it shows God's ability to work good, even from terrible circumstances. Remember that just because the Bible shows something happening, it doesn't mean that God condones it.

Applying the Lesson to Your Own Life

As a teacher of young people it may be hard to imagine a young woman in your group in the same situation as Hagar. Although the exact circumstances of Hagar's pregnancy are uncommon, the idea that a young woman could become pregnant and then left on her own to fend for herself while raising a child is altogether too common in our time. In addition, there is still a significant sex trafficking industry that forces women to have sex with men they do not know or do not love. And this is happening in America, not just other countries.

While Hagar's union with Abraham elevated her to a different status than that of a slave, pregnancy usually doesn't do that in today's society. Becoming pregnant in a loveless relationship could actually make a woman seem less desirable, or even a burden. We know too many single mothers. The fears and joys of love, pregnancy, parenthood, and abandonment are present within this scripture in ways that could touch us deeply or touch our students deeply. We may not even understand some of the reactions we have to the story. Be aware as you prepare for this lesson, how many ancient and modern issues are at play. It is complicated, yet we must deal with it in ways that we might not want to.

The Lesson

Get Started (15 min.)

Option 1: Call to Worship

Begin by singing the song, "Father Abraham."

Some of your students may remember this song from younger years. If not, you can listen to the song on YouTube.

Father Abraham had many sons, and many sons had Father Abraham,
I am one of them, and so are you,
So let's just praise the Lord!

With each verse the group adds a body part to motions including,
Right arm,
Left arm,
Right leg,
Left leg,
and "nod your head."

By the end it is a pretty crazy mess of kids moving around and hopefully still singing the song.

You might explain to the group that the language of the song is all-masculine, even saying that we are all "sons" of Father Abraham. The reason I have chosen this version is not because girls are sons of anyone, but to open a conversation about who Abraham's sons were.

Discussion Question:
- Who were Abraham's seven sons?

If any of them can get more than two, or maybe even more than one, you have some biblical scholars in the room!

Say something like: *Out of Abraham's eight sons, almost all of the discussion of the Bible's attention focuses on the redemption of the promise of God to Abraham through his son Isaac. But Isaac had an older brother, and then six younger brothers. Maybe we have overlooked the older brother in the story, and maybe we should take another look at that older*

Notes:

Leader Tip:
For more information about the seven sons of Abraham, check out Genesis 25:1. In this passage, Abraham takes another wife, Keturah, and she bears him six sons. Turns out the old song should say Father Abraham had eight sons!

brother to see how God might have been working through him as well.

Read a responsive call to worship together

> One: LORD God, you work in ways that we often do not understand. Even when we think we know what you are up to, you can surprise us!
>
> Many: In the story of Abraham, you chose grace when Abraham made mistakes. In the story of Abraham's descendents, you didn't only use one; you used many.
>
> One: Help us to see more clearly into the story of Abraham and his children. Help us to see more clearly into the world of Hagar, the mother of Abraham's first-born.
>
> Girls: Give us eyes to see and hearts to feel what might have gone through Hagar's mind. Open our senses that we may understand her and hear her story, even though she is mostly silent.
>
> Guys: Help us to understand how hard it must have been for Ishmael. Help us to see how scripture has defined him, and how we might see his story anew.
>
> All: Holy One, help us to see in the way you would see, Love in the way you would love, And worship you and learn of you in ways that will please you. Amen.

Option 2: Call to Wake Up

Begin with a classic game of musical chairs. Typically elimination games like this one would be avoided in a setting like this. But the elimination is the point in this illustration. The idea is to help the students begin to understand, in a small and silly way, what it might have been like to be eliminated from the group when Hagar and Ishmael were turned away.

Once you have finished the game, ask those who were eliminated:
- What did it feel like to be eliminated from the game?
- How much fun was it to watch others play while you were out? Was anyone a bit jealous?
- Did anyone think it wasn't really fair?
- Is this type of game a way to understand God's kingdom? Why or why not?

(This is not a way to understand God's kingdom. In God's kingdom, all people are supposed to be included.)

Opening Prayer:
Holy God, help us to see you in everyone, especially those within whom we have a hard time seeing your Spirit. Remind us that all people are your children, and all are created in your image. Help us to hear a familiar story with fresh ears so we can understand something new about you and about how you work in the world during this time of study. Amen.

 ## Listen Up (20 min.)

There is an old comic strip entitled, "Hagar the Horrible." It is a strip about a green skinned witch who is avoided by most everyone, and the silly situations this brings about in her life. The title of this study is, "Hagar the Horrible?" because we often think of the Hagar from the bible as a bad character. She is a home wrecker, coming between Abraham and the woman we consider to be his "legitimate" wife, Sarah. She causes problems in the story because we see the line of Judaism going through Isaac, the son of Abraham and Sarah.

Can we re-see Hagar? Can we see her as something other than a burden in the story or a mistake made by Sarah in trying to fulfill God's promise? Can we instead see Hagar as a person used by God to fulfill God's promise to Abraham?

Read Genesis 16.

Discussion Questions:
- How did Hagar end up having a son with Abraham?
- What were the consequences for Sarah? For Abraham? For Hagar?

In the culture in which these characters lived, women like Hagar had very few options. In a situation like the one Abraham and Sarah were in, one in which they didn't have any offspring of their own to carry on their line, it was considered completely appropriate and legitimate for a slave woman in

Notes:

Notes:

the household to have a child for the wife of the family. Sarah originally intends for this son to be hers— to be raised by her and treated as if he were Sarah and Abraham's biological son. But something happens, and this gives us a clue about what was really going on. When Hagar becomes pregnant, Sarah becomes jealous. Outrageously jealous. Although Sarah had originally intended to have the baby as her son, something changed, and Hagar had become more like a second wife to Abraham. This was a problem. Hagar was now threatening Sarah's place in the family. And with a son of her own, Hagar could have become equal to Sarah or even surpassed her in status.

Something had to be done! The person who should have done something was Abraham. In the ancient middle east, the husband was the leader of the household, so Abraham should have ended the conflict. But instead, he told Sarah to deal with it.

We don't know what Sarah did, but it was severe enough for Hagar to be willing to run away into the wilderness, leaving food, comforts, and the people who had taken care of her in her pregnancy and labor.

When she ran away, she had quite an encounter.

Have someone re-read Genesis 16:7-13.

Have someone read Genesis 15:4-5.

The similarities between the promises given by God are striking! God does not often speak directly to women in writings of the Hebrew Bible, yet in one of the oldest stories we have, God gives Hagar a promise very similar to the one given to Abraham. And this is given to a slave woman who is now a disgraced secondary wife to Abraham! Her offspring will be too numerous to count!

Then another strange thing happens: Hagar gives God a name. She calls God, El-Roi, or "the God who sees me." What a fabulous name for the God who saw and redeemed this poor slave girl who had been rejected by everyone! Then God tells her what the name of her son shall be—Ishmael. This means, "The God who hears."

Discussion Questions:
- What do you think of Sarah's actions in getting a son for Abraham?

- What could Hagar have done to make Sarah so angry once she became pregnant?
- Many Old Testament men have multiple spouses. What was the difference for Sarah when Abraham basically had another wife in Hagar? Was there a difference?
- What could make someone run away into the wilderness without any support, like Hagar did when she was pregnant?
- What do you think of Hagar's encounter with God?

Sarah won the day. In fact, years later when she had a son of her own, she demanded that Hagar and Ishmael be thrown out of Abraham's community. She did not want any rivals for her own son, Isaac.

Have someone read Genesis 21:8-20.

When Hagar and Ishmael were sent away, it distressed Abraham, but he received comfort from God. Similarly, when Hagar was distraught and thought she and Ishmael would not live, an angel of the Lord came and comforted her. The angel gave her water, and confirmed to her that God would make a great nation out of Ishmael.

Discussion Questions:
- How would it feel to be sent out of your home and away from all you knew?
- What do you think Abraham should have done?
- Why did Sarah do what she did? What should she have done?
- Did God fulfill God's promise to Abraham through Ishmael? Why or why not? Is it possible that Abraham's covenant was fulfilled through both Ishmael and Isaac? Or even through all eight of his sons?

Now What? (10 min.)

We often find that the Bible reports, or describes, actions, while it may not necessarily condone them. Even though Hagar seems to be the antagonist in the story of Abraham

Notes:

Just In Case:

Where did Hagar come from?
Genesis 12:10-20

Hagar is described as Sarah's "Egyptian servant." Where would Sarah get an Egyptian servant? In Egypt, of course!

When there was a famine in the land, Abraham and his clan went to Egypt for food. They were welcomed in Pharaoh's palace because Pharaoh had the hots for Sarah. Sarah's relationship with Pharaoh is unclear, but it was enough that Abraham claimed she was his sister, not his wife, so Pharaoh wouldn't kill Abraham to take Sarah away.

For his time with Sarah, Pharaoh gave Abraham a bunch of gifts, including female servants. Abraham's deception got Pharaoh in trouble with God, and when Pharaoh finally figured it out, he sent Abraham away with all the things he had given to Abraham, including his female servants.

and Isaac, we should see that God honors and provides for her. All people are made by God, and all people are God's children. No one is supposed to be left out of the household of God, even though we might have significant differences with them.

Most people, when they look at the story of Hagar, see a problem. Hagar wasn't a problem; she was a beloved child of God, used by God for the fulfillment of God's promises and for the glory of God in the world.

If you played Musical Chairs at the beginning of the session (if you didn't, remind the students that it's a game that eliminates individuals, kind of like the game Sarah was playing with Hagar), set the chairs up again; only this time, let the students know that no one will be out. Instead, at the end of each round, everyone must find a way to be on the chairs that are remaining. At the end, all of the students will somehow be sharing one chair.

Remind the students that we are all in this together; we're all made by God, and God has placed us here with purpose. Sometimes we all end up in a crazy pile in the same chair. Sometimes our plans don't line up with God's. But regardless of our differences, jealousies, or problems, we need to remember that all people are precious in God's sight, and all people belong in our communities. Our job is to care for one another instead of hurting or banishing one another, and this task is to be carried out in our homes and schools, as well as our country and world.

 **Live It (15 min.)**

Discussion Questions:
- Who do we tend to think are outcasts in our lives? Why is this?
- Are there people who want to make us outcasts? Why?
- Who do people want to leave out when they think about the grace of God?

- Even in the Bible text, Hagar seems to be left out. But God was with her; God saved her life and her son's life, and God caused them to be the ancestors of a great multitude. What does that tell us about God?

Close in Prayer. Either ask someone to pray, pray yourself, or use this prayer:

Grace-filled God, we confess that at times we have interpreted your word and your love to be only for us or for people like us. Hagar reminds us that even when people are different, or when we want to make them different and cut them off from ourselves, you are their keeper, and you are their God. Help us to live lives that reflect this by caring for all people, regardless of how they might be different from us, and by doing our best to embody your love for creation. Amen.

Resources Used:
New Interpreter's Study Bible, Abingdon Press, Nashville, TN, 2003; A Journey Through the Hebrew Scriptures, Frances S. Frick, Wadsworth, Toronto, ONT, 2003; The New Interpreter's Bible: A Commentary in Twelve Volumes, Abingdon Press, Nashville, TN, 1998

© 2014 Discipleship Ministry Team of the Ministry Council of the Cumberland Presbyterian Church. All Rights Reserved.

Just In Case:

Ishmael and Isaac
(Show a picture of Jerusalem with the Dome of the Rock and the location of the Ancient Temple.)

It turns out that Ishmael and Isaac were not enemies, as it seems they might have been from the stories we have read. When Abraham died, Ishmael and Isaac buried him together. The tribes even intermarried from time-to-time.

Now days, however, there is much conflict between the people who claim their ancestor to be Ishmael or claim Isaac. There are three major world religions that claim Abraham as their father: Judaism, Islam, and Christianity. Jews and Christians trace that lineage back through Isaac; Muslims trace it through Ishmael. The Holy Land, near where Abraham lived, is constantly in conflict between different groups who claim it to be land given by God to their ancestors.

Can these brothers live in peace?

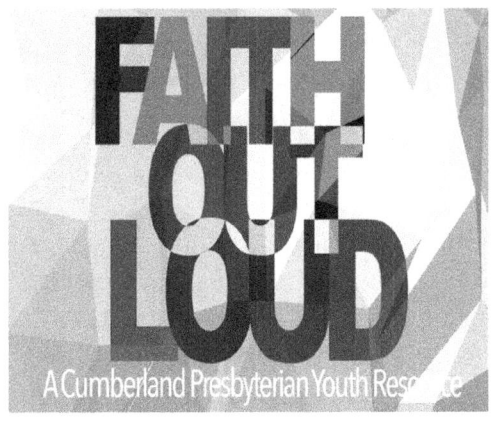

Bathsheba
by Andy McClung

Scripture: 2 Samuel 11:2-5, 14-17, 26-27, and 2 Samuel 12:1-6

Theme: Sin leads to more sin. But when we repent, God forgives.

Resource List

- The song, "If You Want to be Happy for the Rest of Your Life"
- Music player (laptop, iPod, MP3 player, CD player, speakers, etc.)
- Two paper plates for each student
- Markers or crayons

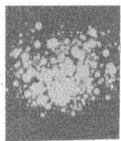

Leader Prep

- Make photocopies of the handout "A Prayer for Forgiveness," one for each student

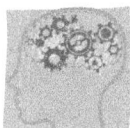

Leader Insight

Connecting to Your Students

Many teens don't like to read the Bible. They see it as outdated, hard to understand, and irrelevant to their lives. But everybody loves a good story. And Bathsheba's story is a good one. There's enough drama, backstabbing, sex, violence, and twists in her story to fuel an entire season of daytime TV talk shows or a primetime drama.

Nobody expects teens to be perfect, but that message isn't always adequately conveyed to church-going teens. They probably hear far more criticism about their behavior than praise. But even if that's not the case, criticism always speaks louder and lingers longer than praise. That's why it's important for them to know that even the heroes of the faith messed up, seriously and often.

It's also important for them to know that God is always ready to forgive us when we mess up. Good Christians aren't perfect, but they're always trying to be more like Christ.

Notes:

Explaining the Bible

Like many women in the Old Testament, Bathsheba is only included to help tell somebody else's (a man's) story. Her role is small but memorable.

When we meet Bathsheba, she's taking a bath. Outside. And David sees her. But Bathsheba wasn't some kind of exhibitionist. Houses in Jerusalem were built around a central courtyard. (Do a web image search for "typical house ancient Jerusalem.") Since David was in the palace, the tallest home around, he would have been able to see into some houses where, with no indoor plumbing, baths were taken. The link between her name and the manner of her introduction is coincidental. "Bath" meant "daughter." So "Bath-Sheba" meant "daughter of an oath."

David found Bathsheba so beautiful he sent somebody to find out who she was. When he learned she was married to someone under his command, he had her brought to him. If she'd been married to someone else, though, probably not much would have changed. David was king; he got what he wanted.

The Bible gives no clue if the sex was consensual. We can't read too much into the use of "he lay with her." This is David's story, so he's the focus. Is it important whether or not David raped Bathsheba? Of course it is. We may be tempted to try and blame Bathsheba for what David did, but a king's words for law, and Bathsheba would most likely not have been able to refuse any request made of her. However, rape or not, David is still most definitely committing adultery.

One sin leads to another. When David found out that his lustful abuse of power had caused Bathsheba to become pregnant, he cooked up a scheme to get out of any responsibility for the child. If Uriah, Bathsheba's husband, thought it was his baby, then this wouldn't be David's problem anymore. Sure Bathsheba would know the truth, but embarrassment would probably keep her quiet.

But Uriah was so loyal to king and country, not to mention God, David's plan failed. Twice. This highlights David's sin. Here's God's anointed King of Israel, and the guy he's trying to dupe is a better man than he is. David's backup plan was to ensure that Uriah died in battle. Then he could take Bathsheba as his wife. He'd be seen as generous instead of adulterous.

Even though we're looking at Bathsheba's story in this lesson, she plays a very passive role in it. We don't know whether or not she consented to sex with David. We don't know how she felt about the pregnancy. We don't know if she mourned Uriah's death (though she probably did). We just see her used like a tool or an object. That should disgust us. David, although he is one of the good guys, is not the good guy in Bathsheba's story.

Bathsheba turns up again in the Bible when David is old and near death (1 Kings). She is still being used by men. In the West (England, Spain, France, etc.), the oldest son of the king inherited the throne. In the Middle East, though, things were different. While a blood relative often was the common successor, pedigree was no guarantee of taking your dad's place as king. The throne went to the most worthy successor.

Adonijah, David's son by another wife, arranged to make it look as if he was chosen to be king after David died. Nathan, however, wanted Solomon, David and Bathsheba's son, to be king. Nathan convinced Bathsheba to ask David to name Solomon as the next king.

Even after David named Solomon as heir, Adonijah wasn't finished. He persuaded Bathsheba to convince Solomon to allow him to marry the late king's nurse, the young, beautiful Abishag… as if she was a consolation prize. Solomon saw through Adonijah's plan. Abishag was important in two ways. First, being married to the late king's wife carried certain legal rights. While Abishag wasn't married to David the two were non-sexually intimate. Having her as his wife might give Adonijah some legal standing to claim the throne. Secondly, she was probably a witness to the dying king naming Solomon heir to the throne. If she was married to Adonijah, he could coerce or force her into saying David named Adonijah instead of Solomon, thus giving him another, albeit slim, chance at the throne.

Was Bathsheba just being conciliatory toward Adonijah, or did she realize his plan and assume Solomon would do away with him? We don't know. What we do know is that Solomon had Adonijah killed, thus ensuring his own hold on the throne was secure.

Bathsheba, used by important men, still gets a place of honor: wife to one king and mother to another king. If her great beauty faded with age, she apparently became smart in the ways of politics to make sure she was always taken care of.

Notes:

Notes:

Theological Underpinnings

God intended women and men to be equal. Genesis says, "Then God said, 'Let us make mankind in our image, in our likeness, so that they may rule over the fish in the sea and the birds in the sky, over the livestock and all the wild animals, and over all the creatures that move along the ground.' So God created mankind in his own image, in the image of God he created them; male and female he created them" (1:26-27 NIV). The Cumberland Presbyterian Confession of Faith says, "In the sight of God, male and female are created equal and complementary" (1.11).

So why do we see all through the Bible, especially in the Old Testament, women treated as less than men? Bathsheba is a prime example. Clearly she was not equal to any of the men in her story, the men who tried to use her to get whatever they wanted. The answer is simple: because we are sinful and do not live as God wants us to live. This sin includes how we treat women or allow women to be treated.

In David we see a God-chosen man who, because he had been given so much, turned into a taker. He took Bathsheba, and then he took her husband's life to cover it up. So, despite some Christian leaders teaching that God wants to give us everything we want so we'll lack nothing and have no struggles in life, God knows that we usually appreciate what we work for and struggle for more than what we are simply given.

Applying the Lesson to Your Own Life

Do you believe in "love at first sight," or is that just another way to refer to lust? Have you ever found someone physically attractive upon first seeing them, but then after getting to know them realized how unattractive their personalities really made them?

Have you ever done something wrong, and then to keep from being discovered you had to do something else wrong? How long did it go on? How did it end? Looking back, do you wish you had owned up to the first sin immediately?

Think of a woman you know only by her association with men: whose mother, or wife, or sister, or employee she is. Do you feel like you know all about her through what you know about the men in her life? Commit to getting to know these women better.

The Lesson

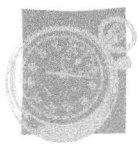

Get Started (10 min.)

Please note that some of the activities included in this lesson may seem to perpetuate sexist attitudes and practices toward women. Actually, however, they are designed to expose the fallacy of such attitudes and practices. With your skillful application of these exercises, this important point will be well made. If a student complains about the apparent sexism, just ask him or her to hang in there for a while.

Play the song, "If You Want to Be Happy for the Rest of Your Life." Jimmy Soul sang the best-known version in 1962, but Rocky Sharpe and the Replays did a very 1980's cover in 1983. It's also on the soundtracks (and in the movies) of 1988's "Clean and Sober," 1990's "Mermaids," and 1997's "My Best Friend's Wedding."

If you're unable to play the song, display and have someone read the lyrics.

Discussion Question:
- What might cause somebody to write a song like this?

Allow answers and comments, but you shouldn't say much.

Discussion Question:
- Who is the most beautiful woman who's ever lived?

Allow answers and some discussion. Throw in your own answer if you wish. If necessary, establish the rule that personality, intelligence, sense of humor, personal interests, abilities, and sense of style don't count; this is strictly about physical beauty. Try to get the entire class to agree on one woman as the most beautiful ever. It's not necessary for everyone to agree, but should make for interesting discussion and highlight that beauty is subjective.

When you've got the list narrowed down, ask the guys only:
- If you were super rich, or king of your own country or something, somehow in a position that gave you tons of power and influence, how far would you go to make (whomever was the top of the list) marry you?
- Would you go so far as to kill her husband and make her marry you? Why/why not?

Notes:

Notes:

Now you get to address the sexism that's been going on. Say something like: *This song, ranking women by their looks alone... how shallow can people get? Women aren't objects to be gawked at, but real persons with interests, personalities, and feelings. And anybody who thinks they're in love with someone after just one look is confusing love with lust (or simply attraction).*

Transition to the lesson by saying: *And that's exactly what happened to King David in the Bible when he saw Bathsheba. She was married to a guy named Uriah, who definitely had not made an ugly woman his wife... and he definitely was not happy for the rest of his life.*

Listen Up (20 min.)

Give each student two paper plates. (The cheapest one you can find will be fine. You can use printer paper instead.) Pass around some markers or crayons as well. Have students write a big "R" on one and a big "NR" on the other.

Have someone read aloud 2 Samuel 11:2-5.

Explain that we don't know exactly what happened between David and Bathsheba. It may or may not have been rape. All we know is that they weren't married, they had sex, and she got pregnant. Announce that you, as a class, will discuss the different possible scenarios implied and decide whether or not each one was a rape. You, as teacher, will describe each scenario and students will vote by holding up "R" for "rape" or "NR" for "not rape" for each one.

Here are the possible scenarios. Read each one; then pause for the vote. Allow students to question each other's answers, but you stay out of the discussion as much as possible.
1. David forced Bathsheba to have sex with him against her will.
2. Because he was king, David ordered Bathsheba to have sex with him. By law she had to do what the king said, so she agreed.

3. David didn't force himself on her or order her to do anything. He just put the moves on her and Bathsheba didn't resist because she knew he had the power to throw her in jail.
4. Bathsheba willingly had sex with David because she was excited that someone as powerful and important as the king was attracted to her.

Now go through the possible scenarios again, one-by-one. This time, "R" means "right," and "NR" means "not right" in the eyes of God. Again, pause for voting and discussion after each scenario. It may be that some of these scenarios aren't technically rape, but none of them is right.

We have no way of knowing exactly what happened, but go ahead and ask students which scenario they think is most likely. Do make students defend/support their answers. Also allow students of differing opinions to debate.

Summarize 2 Samuel 11:6-13, by saying something like: David tried to cover up his sin by cooking up a scheme to make everybody think Bathsheba's husband caused the pregnancy. He called Bathsheba's husband, Uriah, back from the war, saying he wanted news about the battle. Then he sent Uriah home for the night, hoping that he would do what most soldiers do when they go home to their wives after being away. But Uriah didn't cooperate. He was too good a guy. He said as long as his commanding officer, his fellow soldiers, and the Ark of the Covenant weren't spending the night comfortably in their homes, he wouldn't either. So he slept outside.

David tried again the next day, this time getting Uriah drunk and then sending him home to Bathsheba for the night. He probably hoped Uriah would be so drunk he wouldn't remember the night and would end up thinking Bathsheba's baby was his. But again, Uriah was too good a guy to go home.

Have someone read aloud 2 Samuel 11:14-17.

Discussion Question:
- Have you ever done something wrong, and then to keep from getting busted you had to do something else wrong?

Gently encourage answers beyond "yes" and "no" by asking questions such as, "How long did it go on?" "How did it all end?" "Why didn't you feel like you could just stop?" Allow

Notes:

Notes:

time for stories to be shared, and then move on to the following discussion questions.

Discussion Questions:
- So, who is responsible for Uriah's death: David, Joab (Uriah's commanding officer), or the enemy soldiers? Why?
- Isn't David a good guy; is this how good guys act?
- Why would the Jewish people preserve a story that makes one of their greatest heroes look bad? (This is also an interesting point in the debate of whether the Bible is made up or not.)

Have someone read aloud 2 Samuel 11:26-27.

Discussion Question:
- Why do you think Bathsheba agreed to marry David?

Now What? (15 min.)

Explain that God called Nathan, a prophet, to confront David about this whole adultery-turned-to-murder deal. Nathan did so by telling David a story.

Have someone read 2 Samuel 12:1-4.

Discussion Question:
- Do you see what Nathan has done here? What's this story really about?

Explain, if necessary, that David is represented by the rich man of the story. He has plenty of animals, but he's so greedy and self-absorbed he takes the poor man's one, beloved lamb—a female lamb. One that was like a daughter ("bath" = daughter) to him.

Discussion Questions:
- Why didn't Nathan just confront David directly, accusing him of his sins surrounding Bathsheba?

- How much time and energy should Christians spend making sure other people know that what they're doing is sinful and displeasing to God?
- Is Nathan confronting kings from other nations, or the king who agreed to lead God's people?
- Have you ever used your power or influence to take something/ use something that wasn't yours?

Have someone read 2 Samuel 12:5-6.

Explain that once he sees how angry David is at this injustice, Nathan drops the bomb and says, "You're the rich man from the story, David!" Then Nathan confronts David with all the stuff he's been doing that displeases God.

Use the following questions for discussion and reflection. In this portion of the lesson, don't seek or expect immediate answers from your students. Also, don't be afraid to let silence linger while students think about these questions.

Discussion Questions and Reflection:
- Have you ever been angry that somebody did something wrong, but then you realized that you'd been doing pretty much the same thing?
- Have you ever been angry that somebody did something wrong, but then you realized that you're just as guilty of something else just as bad?
- How does God let you, personally, know when you've done something wrong – a guilty conscience, sending someone like Nathan to confront you, a Bible verse that keeps coming up… what?
- When you realize you've sinned, what do you do about it?

Announce that you will ask two more questions. No one is to answer aloud, but there will be two minutes of silence after each question for students to seriously think about their answers. If time is running short reduce this to one minute, but no less.

Refletion Questions:
- Who do you know who is doing something wrong, something that's hurting themselves and/or others, and needs to be confronted about it?
- How can you do like Nathan did, and approach this person in a way that allows them to hear what God wants them to hear?

Just in Case:

One of your students may deduce that David had multiple wives and ask why this was okay back then but not now. You can deflect the question by saying that's not really the focus of this lesson. You can say that even the best people in the Bible did things dishonoring to God, and this is one of them. You can say that the Bible often shows us how things were, not how they were supposed to be. Or you can say that as humans began to understand better and better how God wants us to live, we came to realize that polygamy was not part of that. Polygamy seems to have died out in Judaism sometime during the 400 years between the end of the Old Testament and the beginning of the New Testament. By the time of the New Testament, the practice seems not to have been around in Judaism anymore. And it's never been accepted in Christianity.

DIGGING DEEPER

In 1 Chronicles 3, we find a list of all of David's wives: Ahinoam, Abigail, Maacah, Haggith, Abital, Eglah, and Bathsheba. We also find the names of his sons, born to his wives: Amnon, Daniel, Absalom, Adonijah, Shephatiah, Ithream, Ibhar, Elishua, Elpelet, Nogah, Nepheg, Japhia, Elishama, Eliada, Eliphelet, Shimea, Shobab, Nathan, and Solomon. Finally, we find one daughter: Tamar. Children born to his concubines apparently didn't merit being remembered.

Spend another two minutes in silence. Again, if time is running short reduce this to one minute, but no less.

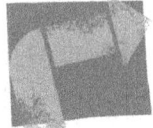

Live It (5 min.)

Say: *God is always willing to forgive those who truly repent of their sins, ask for forgiveness, and honestly seek to live better. What makes David a hero of the faith is not that he always did the right thing, but that when he messed up -- like he did with Bathsheba -- he admitted it, confessed it, asked forgiveness, and tried to do better.*

Explain that after Nathan confronted David about his sins surrounding Bathsheba, David wrote a poem, or song, called a psalm. We can use that psalm as a prayer of confession, a way to repent and seek forgiveness.

Close the class with this or a similar prayer: *Thank you, God for calling us to confess our sins to you. Thank you for always being ready to hear our confessions and grant us forgiveness. Help us to not use people like some people used Bathsheba. Please send people like Nathan into our lives who will help us see when we're sinning.*

Hand out copies of "A Prayer for Forgiveness" from Psalm 51.

Resources used: All the Women of the Bible, by Herbert Lockyer. First and Second Samuel, by Walter Brueggemann. The Interpreter's Bible Vol. II.

© 2014 Discipleship Ministry Team of the Ministry Council of the Cumberland Presbyterian Church. All Rights Reserved.

A PRAYER FOR FORGIVENESS
Psalm 51:1-4, 6-13 (NCV)

*God, be merciful to me
because you are loving.
Because you are always ready to be merciful,
wipe out all my wrongs.
Wash away all my guilt
and make me clean again.
I know about my wrongs,
and I can't forget my sin.
You are the only one I have sinned against;
I have done what you say is wrong.
You are right when you speak
and fair when you judge.*

*You want me to be completely truthful,
so teach me wisdom.
Take away my sin, and I will be clean.
Wash me, and I will be whiter than snow.
Make me hear sounds of joy and gladness;
let the bones you crushed be happy again.
Turn your face from my sins
and wipe out all my guilt.
Create in me a pure heart, God,
and make my spirit right again.
Do not send me away from you
or take your Holy Spirit away from me.
Give me back the joy of your salvation.
Keep me strong by giving me a willing spirit.
Then I will teach your ways to those who do wrong,
and sinners will turn back to you.*

Jezebel
Me, Myself, and I
by Melissa Reid Goodloe

Scripture: 1 Kings 16:30-32, 18:4, 19:1-2, 21:1-25, 2 Kings 9:30-37

Theme: God seeks to be in a relationship with us. When we choose to do evil and sin, we separate ourselves from God— not only in life but also in death. Repentance from sin leads to reconciliation with God.

Resource List

- Markers
- 4 Sheets Newsprint
- Tape
- Anna Calvi's "Jezebel"
- Music player (laptop, iPod, MP3 player, CD player, speakers, etc.)
- Video capability (laptop, projector, DVD player, speakers, etc.)
- Various clips from YouTube

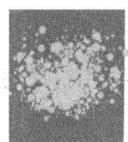

Leader Prep

- Read the scripture, and familiarize yourself with the small passages that mention Jezebel once, as well as the larger ones; both add insight to her character.
- Label newsprint:
  - What characteristics would you look for in a friend/significant other?
  - What would you do if he/she asked you to do something wrong?
  - What would you do if he/she did something wrong to impress you?
- Three movie clips from YouTube
  - "The Godfather:" https://www.youtube.com/watch?v=sY1S34973zA
  - "Mean Girls:" https://www.youtube.com/watch?v=Y_dCc-9pEPM
  - "John Tucker Must Die:" https://www.youtube.com/watch?v=hvn8RCxGauQ

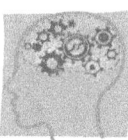

Leader Insight

Connecting to Your Students
Many young people are dating and spending time with their friends and boy/girl friends. There is power in relationships

Notes:

that can cause a person to do things he/she knows are wrong to please others. This lesson helps explore how Jezebel used her power as a woman and a wife to serve Baal and do evil in the sight of the Lord. God seeks a relationship with all of

us if we just repent and give our life to Christ. Some of your young people may feel they have sinned to the point that God would want nothing to do with them. Nobody is beyond redemption, unless they choose to deny God's gift of salvation. Jezebel denied God until the end and was met with a horrible fate.

Explaining the Bible

Jezebel is mentioned several times in the Bible, and none of it is positive. Jezebel was the daughter of Ethbaal, a priest of a god named Baal. Ethbaal, the priest and King of Tyre, murdered his own brother to take over the throne. Jezebel followed in her father's footsteps and was herself a power-hungry murderess who stopped at nothing to get what she wanted.

Ahab, a weak, self-pitying man, was the king of Israel at the time, and he renounced his authority to his bride, the princess Jezebel. In spite of God's laws forbidding idolatry and the worship of any god but Jehovah, Ahab married this princess who brought with her to Israel hundreds of priests of Baal. Jezebel was such a dictator that she soon became master and ruler over her husband, the king.

From the day she said "I do" until the day she died, Jezebel worshiped Baal and did evil in the sight of the Lord. We know nothing of her upbringing except that she was the daughter of a king who also worshiped Baal.

Jezebel used her feminine wiles to aid her in manipulating the men around her. She was driven by greed and jealousy. The examples we see show a strong woman who did not like to be challenged. She was driven by a need to be in control. Her husband, though a king, was weak. She was able to convince him to do what she wanted. She also committed horrible acts in order to please her husband.

Jezebel had prophets of God killed because they objected to her lifestyle; she had an innocent vineyard owner killed because her husband desired the vineyard; and she threatened Elijah's life for killing the prophets of Baal. She never sought God in her life no matter the many warnings given to her.

Jezebel's death was proclaimed by the Lord through Elijah in 1 Kings 21:23; He said that she would be eaten by dogs. On the day of her death, she stood at the window after fixing her hair and makeup. Her own servants threw her to her death, and the dogs ate her flesh, fulfilling the prophesy and leaving nothing but her skull.

Jezebel's end was not a pretty one, more gruesome than most, perhaps as an object lesson to all who set themselves up against the one true God. Her thirty years of tyranny over Israel ended. The terror visited upon Jezebel was a testimony to the Israelites, and to us, that God's power is supreme, and those who consistently defy Him invite disaster and death into their lives.

Theological Underpinnings
During a time when women were not considered powerful, Jezebel proves there is power in beauty and cunning. She uses this power to her advantage. Some people want to please others and are willing to sacrifice their character to achieve popularity. Girls need to learn that beauty and intelligence, though not sins, should not be used for selfish gain. Guys need to learn that they should not be swayed by a pretty face. We were each made in God's image, and each of us is unique.

God is all powerful. There are many examples that prove God's power. There are those who worship other gods, and their power fails when tested.

God seeks a relationship with each of us. Jezebel and her husband chose to do evil in the sight of the Lord. If they had chosen to change their ways, God would have reconciled them to himself. There are many examples of people who have lived a sinful lifestyle and then chose to follow God's will. No one has sinned to the point that God does not desire to reconcile with him/her.

Applying the Lesson to Your Own Life
"Jezebel" is a name synonymous with evil; she is the epitome of the wicked woman. So infamous is her name that, to this day, to call a woman a "Jezebel" is a very great insult.

Have you ever acted inappropriately or been mean to someone and regretted it later? How did you correct the situation? How did you repair the damage done?

Notes:

Notes:

Have you ever felt you sinned to the point that God would want nothing to do with you?

Know that whatever happened in your past is in your past. Christ' resurrection was enough. Your repentance was enough. You are enough. Reflect on that promise as you

prepare for this lesson. That may be the most important word our young people hear. God's love is constant.

The Lesson

Get Started (15 min.)

Say: *Today we are talking about Jezebel and the pressures our friends, significant others, and even we place on our relationship with God.*

List on newsprint the following questions:

- What characteristics would you look for in a friend/significant other?
- What would you do if he/she asked you to do something wrong?
- What would you do if he/she did something wrong to impress you?

Have students go around the room and answer the questions on newsprint.

Have Anna Calvi's "Jezebel" playing as students answer the questions.

Ask:
- When you hear the name Jezebel or someone called Jezebel, what comes to mind?

Listen Up (20 min.)

Say: *You may have heard the name Jezebel. How many have read her story? (Pause for response.) Today we are going to read Jezebel's account in the book of 1 Kings.*

Have students take turns reading the following scripture passages aloud. Between each scripture passage, have students share actions from each passage that go against God's will. Write these on newsprint or a dry-erase board.

- 1 Kings 16:30-32
- 1 Kings 18:4
- 1 Kings 19:1-2
- 1 Kings 21:1-25
- 2 Kings 9:30-37

Once all scriptures are read and the actions are recorded, have each student describe Jezebel in three words or less.

Discussion Questions:
- What are the most interesting moments in Jezebel's story?
- In the story, who acts? Who gets what they want? If you were in the story, which person would you want to be friends with? Which person would you want to avoid?
- Do you automatically judge someone by the way they look?
- In our society, appearance is very important. How do you think Jezebel would be viewed in our society?
- Can you think of leaders or celebrities that remind you of Jezebel? How so?
- What is God's interaction with the main characters? What does this tell you about the narrator's image of God? Do you agree with this image?
- What is happening on either side of the story, in the chapters before and after it? Does this help you understand what is happening?
- Are the characteristics and actions of the people in the story still present in the world? How is the story relevant to your own life?

Notes:

Notes:

Now What? (10 min.)

What Power Does to People?

Show the clip suggested for each film listed: "The Godfather," "Mean Girls," and "John Tucker Must Die." Each of the clips come from films about the balance of power. In each film, power corrupts.

- "The Godfather:" power corrupts the whole family, through the generations. https://www.youtube.com/watch?v=sY1S34973zA
- "Mean Girls:" Regina George rules the school as the "Queen Bee." https://www.youtube.com/watch?v=Y_dCc-9pEPM
- "John Tucker Must Die:" A guy who dates three different girls at the same time and thinks he is invincible. https://www.youtube.com/watch?v=hvn8RCxGauQ

After the clips have been shown, ask the following questions. Jot responses down on newsprint or a dry-erase board.

- What are the main ideas in any story that has a "Jezebel" character?
- What are Jezebel's qualities? Her strengths? Her weakness?
- What are the main ideas in these films?
- What are the central relationships?
- Do any of the scenes remind you of your own life or experiences?
- How can we reach out to the Jezebels in our life, yet remain true to what God has called us to do?

Optional Activity: Jezebel on Trial

Conduct a mock trial of Jezebel to decide if her death was justified by her actions. You will need a panel of judges, a prosecution, a defense lawyer, assistants, and gatherers of evidence.

The question at hand: Did Jezebel deserve the death she received?

Do the following:
- Nominate a small panel of jurors to decide the case of Jezebel and her death.

- Divide into two groups, one for the defense and one for the prosecution.
  - o Have each group decide on points their lawyer will argue, and imagine points that the other side's lawyer may raise.
  - o Choose a member of the group who will speak as a lawyer for its side, and his/her assistants.
- Nominate a panel of judges, and decide on their role.
- Conduct the trial with an opening address, arguments for both sides, and summary.
- Listen to feedback from the panel of judges and the jury

Live It (5 min.)

Say: *Prayer is an important part of strengthening our relationship with God. Let's join together in saying this prayer: God, we want to know you. We ask for forgiveness for our sins, and we want to live more like you. Thank you that you forgive our sins. We thank you for the good friends you place in our lives. Help us to distance ourselves from those who take us away from you. Amen*

Resources used: http://www.gotquestions.org/life-Jezebel.html, CEO, S. Michael Houdmann.

© 2014 Discipleship Ministry Team of the Ministry Council of the Cumberland Presbyterian Church. All Rights Reserved.

Notes:

Prisca / Priscilla
by Andy McClung

Scripture: Acts 18:1-3, 18:18-19, 18:24-28, Romans 16:3-4, 1 Corinthians 16:19, 2 Timothy 4:19, Galatians 2:20, Colossians 3:17

Theme: Being famous (or popular) isn't as important as we think. Serving God is more important than we think.

Resource List

- A toy car
- 2-4 songs (Leader Prep)
- Display lyrics to chosen songs
- Music player (laptop, iPod, MP3 player, CD player, speakers, etc.)
- (Optional) Video capability (laptop, projector, DVD player, speakers, etc.)

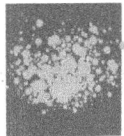

Leader Prep

- Have at least one or two songs and/or music videos from each group.

  Group One songs
  - "Rockstar," by Nickelback
  - "Jukebox Hero," by Foreigner
  - "The Cover of the Rolling Stone," by Dr. Hook

  Group Two songs
  - "Turn the Page," by Bob Seeger
  - "The Load Out," by Jackson Browne
  - "Into the Great Wide Open," by Tom Petty (this one is much more effective if showing music videos)
  - "Shooting Star," by Bad Company

- Locate lyrics, and display them for the chosen songs.

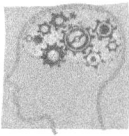

Leader Insight

Connecting to Your Students
Ever since there have been celebrities, teens have dreamed of becoming famous. But nowadays, a lot of teens expect to become famous. Maybe it's because they've repeatedly seen

> **Leader Tip:**
> The trend today is to give equal weight to everyone's opinion, and therefore everyone's advice. To read why this isn't always wise, web search, "The Death of Expertise," by Tom Nichols.

unknown persons propelled into the spotlight through "reality" TV shows and YouTube, even though that spotlight may be very short-lived. Maybe it's because of the rampant loneliness in contemporary US society. Maybe it's because they've already participated in multiple "graduation" ceremonies before even entering high school. Maybe it's because they "won" a trophy just for paying the league fee and showing up at the games. Maybe it's because their parents, educators, and the "edutainment" industry have given them an overinflated sense of entitlement and self-esteem through a barrage of "everybody is special" messages.

Anyone who follows Christ and loves these children should be appalled by this obsessive desire for fame.

Explaining the Bible
JIn 2005, author Jake Halpern visited a convention for aspiring child actors and models. He was shocked when, mistaking him for a talent agent, the children and their parents threw themselves at him. He says, "The beggar children of Bombay weren't as fierce or as desperate." Intrigued, Halpern, with the aid of Syracuse University, conducted a study. Halpern discovered that American teens are obsessed with fame. Twice as many girls would rather be famous than be a university president; three times as many would rather be a celebrity's personal assistant than a US Senator; and four times as many would rather be famous than be CEO of a major company. Over 25% of the teens, of both genders, believed fame would make them happier and more loved. In the question, "Who would you most like to have dinner with," Jesus lost out to Jennifer Lopez.

Halpern's overall findings included:
- Teens would rather be famous than smart.
- African-American teens are more desperate for fame than other races.
- Teens who follow celebrity news want and expect fame the most, and they expect fame to improve their lives.
- Lonely teens are more likely to follow celebrity news and believe fame will solve their problems.
- Teens believe that famous people deserve their fame.

Psychologist Joseph White says this obsession comes from inner loneliness caused by so many families falling apart, which denies children of love, attention, and support. He says the average American has half as many close relationships as ten years ago. Fame, then, is seen as a shortcut to get what we're meant to get through meaningful relationships.

Ralph Martin, an expert in making church relevant to real life, says this obsession with fame comes from spiritual emptiness. "People are grasping for love, for attention, for being valued, because they're missing the security that comes from knowing they are eternally loved and valued by God." But fame, he says, won't do it because what people are looking for only has real value when it comes from God.

This desire for praise is innate, and not necessarily a bad thing. The desire to be awesome at something is healthy. The desire to help a talented person do something great is admirable. The problem is teens don't want to be famous for doing something great. They just want to be famous, they want it fast, and they expect it to come easily. They don't want to spend years in their garage developing software to become the next Bill Gates; they want to "be discovered" and become the next Paris Hilton overnight.

Compare all this with Priscilla. What we know about her tells us she could have been a celebrity in the Early Church. But we don't know much about her because everything she did was for God's glory, not her own.

Priscilla's real name was Prisca; "Priscilla" is the diminutive form. In scripture she is called Prisca by Paul, and Priscilla by Luke. She was married to Aquila and the two are always mentioned together.

This couple is mentioned six times in the Bible, and Priscilla is mentioned first four of those times. This was highly unusual and may indicate that she was more prominent in the Church.

We don't know much about Priscilla. She was Jewish. She was from Rome, moving to Corinth when Emperor Claudius forced all Jews out of Rome in A.D. 49. (This would have made her one of the earliest Christian converts living in Rome.) She was a tent-maker. She sailed with Paul from Corinth to Ephesus and helped start the church there, which met in her home. (All the early churches met in their leaders' homes). She also taught a prominent, popular, and eloquent preacher named Apollos a deeper faith. Apollos was already popular because of his eloquence, but his faith was shallow because he had not received the baptism of the Holy Spirit. Priscilla, realizing the danger of a shallow-faith preacher, taught him a deeper faith.

Today Priscilla is a saint in the Roman Catholic Church. Leg-

Notes:

Notes:

end says that she returned to Rome at some point and chose torture and death over worshiping a god besides God. She's buried in one of the first catacombs in Rome, and it was named after her. There's also a church in Rome named after her. She is suspected by some to be the author of Hebrews. Someone whom Paul praised so highly and who was so influential in the early Church could have easily milked her fame for all it was worth. Maybe we know so little about Priscilla because she understood that earthly fame isn't worth much, but glorifying God is worth everything.

Theological Underpinnings

Humility is having a proper sense of one's own importance. Pride is just the opposite—having an exaggerated sense of one's own importance. From the beginning of Christianity, humility has been upheld as a virtue, and pride has been recognized as a sin.

Humility leads to strong and healthy relationships with God and other people. Pride leads to further sin, and isolation from both God and other people.

When we read Genesis 3, we may be tempted to say that the first sin committed by humans was disobeying God by eating that forbidden fruit. The first sin, however, really came before that disobedient act. Yes, disobeying God's command was a sin, but pride was the sin that led to eating the forbidden fruit. Adam and Eve had an exaggerated sense of their own importance, thinking that they knew better than God what was best for them. So pride was the first sin.

When explaining what disrupted the perfect relationship God had established with humankind, our Confession of Faith puts Adam and Eve's "rejecting their dependence on God" before their "willful disobedience" (2.03). Thinking that one can rely on oneself rather than God is an exaggerated sense of one's abilities and importance, and thus is pride.

Applying the Lesson to Your Own Life

Do you think a "Hollywood Minute" is worthwhile in news broadcasts? Do you know more about the personal lives of some celebrity couples than your own neighbors or relatives? Do you pay more attention to American Idol than the news? If you said yes to any of these… why?

How much time and money do you spend keeping up with celebrities (reading "People" or "Us Magazine", watching "Entertainment Tonight," clicking on web links, etc.)? Do you think such things make the consumer a better person and make the world a better place? If so, how? If not, then why do them? Could such an interest be harmful?

Did you want to be famous when you were a teen? If so, what would you now say to your younger self about such a desire? If not, what made you different from so many teens today?

The Lesson

Get Started (10 min.)

Keep the toy car hidden.

Use your best game show host voice to welcome your students to a new game show, "Celebrity Quiz." Announce that today's grand prize is (dramatic pause)... A NEW CAR!

Explain the rules: students will go head-to-head and answer questions about celebrities. The winner gets to go again. The loser sits down. Whoever answers the most questions overall wins the grand prize.

Select two students to "face off" in front of the class.

The first to give the correct answer to your question will be the winner and will get to stay. The loser has to sit down. The only answers you can accept are the ones printed below. If you have a small class, it's fine for students to have more than one turn. The overall winner is whoever correctly answers the most questions, so have someone keep track.

Ask: *She was eventually Secretary of State. She ran for president. She was a US senator. But what was Hillary Clinton first famous for?* [Correct answer: Being married to President Bill Clinton.]

Whoever answers correctly first is the winner and remains

Notes:

Notes:

Leader Tip:
If you have more students than questions listed, research your own "before they were 'famous'" questions.
Total up everyone's scores and present the "new car" to the winner.

---

standing. The loser sits down. You select another player.

Ask: *He has released an album. He was in a couple of movies. But what was Kevin Federline (K-Fed) first famous for?* [Correct answer: Being married to Britney Spears.]

Ask: *Before she was in a reality TV show, what was Paris Hilton famous for?* [Correct answer: Being famous/Being a celebrity/The descendent of the founder of Hilton Hotels.]

Whoever answers correctly first is the winner and remains standing. The loser sits down. You select another player.

Ask: *Before they were in a reality TV show, what were the Kardashian sisters famous for?* [Correct answer: Being famous/Being a celebrity/Daughters of a celebrity.]

Whoever answers correctly first is the winner and remains standing. The loser sits down. You select another player.

Ask: *Is it possible to become famous for doing nothing?* [Correct answer: Yes.]

Whoever answers correctly first is the winner and remains standing. The loser sits down. You select another player.

Ask: *What's more important, being famous or serving God?* [Correct answer: Serving God.]

Transition to the lesson by saying something like: *Sometimes it seems like famous people have it great. Everybody loves them. Everybody wants to be around them. They're rich. The same is true with being popular, which is being "famous" on a smaller scale. But the truth is, there are other things far more important than being famous.*

Listen Up (20 min.)

Tell your student this story: *On October 15, 2009, the attention of the world was on southeast Colorado when it was reported that a six-year-old boy had accidentally taken flight in some kind of homemade balloon all by himself. Everyone was worried for his safety and watched the news to find out if he would be rescued. Police helicopters were scrambled. The Denver airport was shut down. Authorities finally spotted the flying balloon. News trucks and choppers followed it, filming the whole time. When it landed it was empty, so a search began for the boy's body. The fear was that he had fallen out of the balloon at some point. Two hours later the sheriff announced that the boy was safe and at home. He had been hiding in a box in the attic the whole time and had never been in the balloon. It was all a mistake.*

Explain that you are going to ask a question and your students are to indicate their answer by moving to one side of the room or the other. This is forced choice: students must choose one of the answers offered. No one may stay in the middle.

Discussion Question:
- Do you think this was a hoax, perpetrated by the boy's parents in an attempt to become famous?

Now indicate one side of the room for those who say "Yes," and the other side for those who say "No." Have students move to indicate their answers.

Hopefully, there will be a mix of answers. If so, or if everyone answers "No," proceed as explained below. If, however, everyone answers "Yes," ask students, one by one, why they think this was an attempt to become famous. When all students have answered, say that you will share some more details. Students may change their answers at any time. When students are 100% sure their answer is right, they should sit down. Share the details one by one until everyone is sitting down.

If you have a mix of answers at first, explain that you will share some more details. Students may change their answers at any time. Keep sharing details until you run out or everyone has gathered on the "hoax" side of the room.

Notes:

Notes:

Details:
- The little boy's name was Falcon.
- The balloon was shaped like a UFO.
- The parents met at an acting school in Hollywood.
- The dad was an amateur scientist, and on national TV said he designed and built the balloon.
- To report his son missing and possibly in danger, the dad called the local news station before calling 911.
- Before this incident, the parents had applied to, auditioned for, and been on the reality TV show, "Wife Swap."
- Before this incident, the parents had attempted to, and failed, to get their own reality TV show produced.
- Falcon, when asked on live TV why he didn't come out of the attic when his family and police were calling his name during the search, said to his parents, "You said we had to do this for the show."
- The parents were charged with felonies. The mom admitted that it was all a stunt to make the family more attractive to producers for their reality show. Both parents plea-bargained, served a short time in jail, paid hefty fines, and were put on probation.

Discussion Questions:
- Is it worth it? Is it worth lying to the world, making your children lie to police and reporters, and going to jail... just to be famous for a little while?
- How far would you go, what would you do, what would you risk, to be famous?

Say: *A long time ago there was a woman named Priscilla who could have been very famous, but she chose to do something better.*

Have someone read aloud Acts 18:1-3.

Say: *"Priscilla" is the short version of "Prisca." She is called by both names in scripture. Her name is only mentioned six times in the whole Bible, and she is always mentioned alongside her husband Aquila. But in four of those six places, her name is mentioned first. It was unusual back then for the wife to be named first, so we think she may have been more prominent or influential than her husband in the early church.*

Have someone read aloud Acts 18:18-19.

Say: *Priscilla and Aquila were friends and co-workers in ministry with Paul. They went with him on a trip. Priscilla and*

Aquila stopped in Ephesus, but Paul kept going. It is believed that Priscilla and Aquila started the church there in Ephesus. This is the church to which Ephesians was later written.

Have someone read aloud Acts 18:24-28.

Say: *There was this guy named Apollos who was really "on fire for the Lord." He was a popular preacher, but his faith was shallow. When Priscilla and Aquila heard him preach they knew he could do a lot of good for Christianity, but they also knew that with a shallow faith he could do a lot of damage. So they taught him and led him to a deeper faith in Christ. And they were right; he did do a lot of good.*

Explain that Prisca/Priscilla is mentioned three more times in the Bible—Romans 16:3, 1 Corinthinas 16:19, and 2 Timothy 4:19. These are just Paul adding to the end of a letter—"Prisca and Aquila say hello," or "Say hello to Prisca and Aquila for me." It is very significant, though, for Priscilla to be mentioned in Paul's letters. It indicates that he and many others in the early church knew her well.

Discussion Question:
- So, if Priscilla was so important in the early church, why do you think we know so little about her?

Allow responses. Affirm anything reasonable with "Good thought," "Yes, maybe so," or "You could be right." If no student says it, be sure to conclude the speculation with: *Maybe we know so little about Priscilla because she understood that earthly fame isn't worth much, but glorifying God is worth everything.*

Discussion Question:
- Does anybody know who Brad Renfro is?

Brad Renfro was an unknown twelve-year-old from Tennessee who got cast in a lead role in the 1994 movie, "The Client." The movie was a big hit and Brad became famous. Soon he was in trouble with drugs, the law, and his career. He died of a drug overdose at the age of 26.

Discussion Questions:
- What do you think of when I say the names Miley Cyrus… Lindsay Lohan… Mike Tyson?

Allow responses, then say: *These are all big celebrities who were super-famous and who made tons of money, but ended*

Notes:

Notes:

up in really bad situations because of their fame. And the list goes on and on and on and on.

Now What? (15 min.)

For this portion of the lesson, you will need to obtain at least two songs, preferably more..

Don't reveal this to your students, but there are two groups of songs here: one more focused on the fantasy of being a celebrity, and one more focused on the reality. You will show/play one or more song(s) from the first group, and then ask students to say what they think being famous would be like. Then you'll show/play one or more song(s) from the second group and ask the same question.

Display the lyrics for the songs you plan to use so students can read along as the song plays, or have them for reference during the discussion.

Play one or two songs from Group One, then say: *Using just one or two words, describe what you think life would be like as a celebrity.* Write down some of the words.

Group One songs
- "Rockstar," by Nickelback
- "Jukebox Hero," by Foreigner
- "The Cover of the Rolling Stone," by Dr. Hook

Play one or two songs from Group Two, and then say: *Using as many words as you wish, describe what you think life would be like as a celebrity.* As students respond, compare what they say now with their brief responses from a minute ago.

Group Two songs
- "Turn the Page," by Bob Seeger
- "The Load Out," by Jackson Browne
- "Into the Great Wide Open," by Tom Petty (this one is much more effective if showing music videos)

- "Shooting Star," by Bad Company

If you have time, discuss what they heard in the songs. Possible discussion points:
- How many songs mentioned casual sex or drugs? Who is more likely to be drawn to the promise of casual sex and drug use—people who feel good about themselves or people who are insecure and lonely?
- Can people be addicted to fame?
- Why do you think so many people believe being famous will solve their problems?
- Did any of the songs make you feel like the singers wished they were just playing music for fun instead of to be famous?
- What do you think, "Don't you know that you are a shooting star" means? What's a shooting star do?

Live It (5 min.)

Say: *The desire to be famous, or even just popular, is a strong temptation. But Priscilla lived a better way, a way the Bible tells us to live. Galatians 2:20 says, "It is no longer I who live, but Christ who lives within me." And Colossians 3:17 says, "Whatever you do, in word or deed, do everything in the name of the Lord Jesus, giving thanks to God the Father through him."*

Say: *Fame is addictive. Fame fades. Fame corrupts. Fame dehumanizes. Fame paints a target on the famous. In the end, fame isn't all that important. But serving God is eternally important.*

Resources used: azlyrics.com. denverpost.com. freerepublic.com. jakehalpern.com. The New Bible Dictionary

© 2014 Discipleship Ministry Team of the Ministry Council of the Cumberland Presbyterian Church. All Rights Reserved.

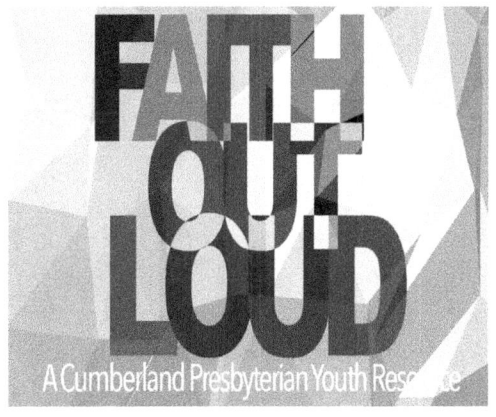

Lydia
by Andy McClung

Scripture: Acts 16:6-15

Theme: Accepting Christ is just the beginning of the Christian journey. Living according to Christ's plan continues the journey.

Resource List

- Map of "Bible lands" or the Middle East
- Lots of index cards (five or six per student)
- A pen for each person
- A bag or bucket
- Enough space for the class to spread out in small groups
- Bulletin board and pushpins, or a wall
- Painters or masking tape
- (Optional) Lyrics to "We are One in the Spirit"

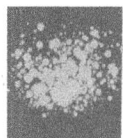

Leader Prep

- Before class, find online and print the following photos:
    - A Jewish person wearing a yarmulke (the little black skull cap), and/or a Hassidic Jew with the black hat and curls
    - A Muslim woman with everything but her eyes covered in the shapeless dress, and/or a Muslim man wearing a taqiyah (the little knit skull cap) and a bushy beard
    - A Hindu woman with the dot on her forehead
    - A Buddhist monk with the bald head and orange robe

If your church was around in the 50's or 60's, there are probably some large, color maps of the "Bible Lands" in a closet or classroom. If so, find the one labeled "Paul's Missionary Journeys," and use it during this lesson to point out the places mentioned in Acts 16. (Find Crete in the middle of the Mediterranean Sea, and go north into the Aegean Sea. All places mentioned are to the east and northwest of it.) Many study Bibles also have similar maps in the back.

- (Optional) Dress in purple for this class meeting. For extra fun, ask students to wear something purple, or decorate the room in purple.

Notes:

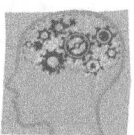

Leader Insight

Connecting to Your Students
Many church-going teens have grown up seeing their parents and other adults compartmentalize their faith. They go to church on Sundays and, maybe, Wednesdays. They may attend a Sunday school class or small group. They don't hide the fact that they're Christians, but it'd be hard for an observer to know it by watching how they do their jobs or live their lives throughout the week. Their faith barely influences how they live. Their Christianity is compartmentalized to church and church-related places and events. The rest of the time, they live just like everyone else.

What we see or experience regularly becomes normalized. Teens who have witnessed their parents and other adults compartmentalizing their Christianity grow to think it's normal. The truth is, however, that if a person's faith is worth anything at all, it should greatly affect every aspect of their life. There's no such thing as a part-time Christian.

Explaining the Bible
Lydia may not have been Lydia's name. Lydia is also the name of a city in the region called Thyatira, part of what we know today as Turkey. That's the region the woman named Lydia was from. When Luke wrote Acts, he may have originally identified her as "The Lydian," a name for someone from that region, and this was translated as the proper name, "Lydia." If this is so, we don't know if Luke gave her that designation or if that was how she was already known. Of course, it may be that she was from Lydia and her name was Lydia. Surely there are a few Savannahs from Savannah, Dallases from Dallas, and Londons from London.

Most of what we know about Lydia comes from reading between the lines because there just isn't very much information about her in the Bible.

We do know that she was the first recorded Christian convert in Europe. And we can deduce that this wasn't the only way she was a trailblazer. Acts 16:14 says she was "a dealer in purple cloth." This means she was a businesswoman in a time when the vast majority of women were homemakers. No mention is made of her husband, so she might have been a single, or widowed, woman who was earning a living for herself in a time when most widows had to beg. It's mentioned that she had "a household" which, in the Bible, usually means a person's family and servants or slaves. Only rich people had servants or slaves, so Lydia may have been well off when most people were barely getting by. We know she believed in the one true, living God, when most people in her area believed in made-up gods. From all this we get a picture of Lydia as a strong, independent, faithful, and smart woman. Lydia's story, at least the part we know, starts with Paul. He and Silas were traveling around, teaching people about Jesus, and starting churches everywhere they could. They wanted to go into Asia, but God said not to. (This was the far western portion of Asia, called Asia Minor, part of what we call the Middle East today.) And then Paul had a vision of a man from Macedonia – which was in the opposite direction of where Paul wanted to go – asking Paul to come help them there. Paul and Silas went west to Macedonia, which is north of Greece. They ended up in Philippi, a major city in Macedonia.

Although Jewish people had spread all over the world, there must not have been very many around Philippi. There was no synagogue there. The rule was that there had to be ten Jewish men in a community to start a synagogue. So the people who worshipped the real God – instead of the many Greek or Roman gods – just gathered at the riverside every Sabbath to worship. Either this was standard practice for towns without a synagogue, or Paul asked around, for Paul and Silas knew where to go on the Sabbath Day.

The only other worshipers they found there were women. Lydia was one of these women. Luke calls her "a worshiper of God," meaning that she was Jewish in faith. But having been born in Thyatira, she might have been ethnically Gentile. Paul started teaching, and God worked through that teaching to call Lydia to follow Christ.

Lydia's first act as a brand-new Christian was to practice the gift of hospitality. She invited those traveling missionaries to stay at her house. Later on, after God breaks Paul and Silas out of prison with an earthquake, the first place they go is back to Lydia's house.

It's highly likely that the church Paul started there in Philippi met in Lydia's house. It's probable that when Paul later wrote a letter to that church, which we call the Epistle to the Philippians, Lydia was still leading that church. So even though he wrote the letter to the church as a whole, Paul may very well

Notes:

Notes:

have had Lydia in mind when he wrote, "I thank my God every time I remember you, constantly praying with joy in every one of my prayers for all of you, because of your sharing in the gospel from the first day until now" Philippians 1:3-5 (NRSV).

And remember how Lydia's name might not have been Lydia? In Philippians 4:2, Paul speaks directly to two women of the Philippian church: Euodia and Syntyche. Could one of them have been the woman we know as Lydia?

Theological Underpinnings

One thing that distinguishes Cumberland Presbyterians from some other Christians is that we believe God initiates a person's coming to Christ. God does this through the activity of the Holy Spirit, working through scripture, the sacraments, corporate worship, the ministries of believers, and in other ways we humans can't understand. God calls a sinful person to repentance before the sinner has any desire to repent. (See our Confession of Faith 4.01-4.03.) So for Cumberland Presbyterians, it's not "I have decided to follow Jesus;" it's "God has called me to follow Jesus, and I have responded with a 'Yes.'" In Acts 16:14, we see this truth in Lydia's conversion story: God "opened her heart" to the teaching of Paul and Silas.

In Cumberland Presbyterian theology, the Holy Spirit then moves us from being believers to being disciples—that is, from simply believing to acting on those beliefs. We call this sanctification (Confession 4.21-4.23). Sanctification is God setting believers apart from other humans to serve God and other people. Lydia gets there more quickly than most. She immediately offers Christian hospitality to Paul and Silas. Soon thereafter, she opens her home to be the place where the new Philippian Church meets.

Hospitality is just one Christian behavior that sanctification produces. As we continue to grow in grace by learning, serving, and listening, God gives us new gifts and strengthens those already given.

Applying the Lesson to Your Own Life

Is there a "Shepherd's Guide" phonebook for your community? These directories list only Christian-owned businesses. The idea is for Christians to support other Christians—call a Christian plumber, buy from a Christian florist. That way, assuming those business owners tithe, you'll be supporting all sorts of ministry with the money you spend.

Do you think this is a good idea? Would you trust a business listed in this guide more than another business? Would it be better to do business with non-Christians and thus have a chance to share the gospel?

Do you compartmentalize your faith, or do you find ways to live out your faith in your everyday life and career?

Which does your personal ministry focus on more: helping people hear God's call to salvation, or deepening the discipleship of believers? Why? Which does your congregation's ministry focus on more? Your presbytery? Our denomination?

The Lesson

Get Started (10 min.)

Have a map of Paul's missionary journeys on hand.

Share the following photos with the class:
- A Jewish person wearing a yarmulke (the little black skull cap), and/or a Hassidic Jew with the black hat and curls
- A Muslim woman with everything but her eyes covered in the shapeless dress, and/or a Muslim man wearing a taqiyah (the little knit skull cap) and a bushy beard
- A Hindu woman with the dot on her forehead
- A Buddhist monk with the bald head and orange robe

Hold up the photos on at a time, and ask:
- What religion is this person?

When you've gone through all your photos, say: *You could tell all these people's religions just by looking at them. How would you know if someone is a Christian just by looking at them?*

Spend some time on this. Crosses on jewelry don't really count because lots of people wear crosses as a fashion state-

Notes:

Notes:

Leader Tip:
While reading the Bible aloud should always be taken seriously – this is God speaking to us – we should never discourage anyone from reading because they might mispronounce a name. If a reader messes up, just say, "That's a hard one," and offer the proper pronunciation. If there's laughter, redirect it from being toward the reader to the "weird" word itself.

---

ment rather than a religious symbol; cross tattoos would also fall into this category. Seeing someone in church or reading the Bible doesn't count because anybody can walk into a church or pick up a Bible. A clergy robe might count, but without the stole they look much like judicial or academic robes. Besides, no minister wears a robe outside of church. A clerical collar would count, of course, but you're trying to focus on all Christians, not just clergy.

After some discussion, if no one offers this answer, say: *It should be easy to spot a Christian who is really living as a Christian, because in many ways, those who follow Christ will be acting differently from everyone else.*

(Optional) If your class is musical, this would be a great time to sing "We are One in the Spirit."

Listen Up (15 min.)

Have someone read aloud Acts 16:6-15. Warn the reader ahead of time that there are some hard-to-pronounce place names. Suggest these pronunciations:
- Phrygia (FRIH-jee-uh)
- Galatia (guh-LAY-shee-uh)
- Mysia (MIS-ee-uh)
- Macedonia (mas'uh-DOH-nee-uh)
- Troas (TROH-az)
- Samothrace (SAM-oh-thrays)
- Neapolis (nee-A-puh-lis)
- Philippi (FIH-luh-pi')
- Thyatira (thi'uh-TI-ruh)

Say: *There are three things that stand out in Lydia's story. First, she was a woman. Second, her story reveals that it's God who initiates conversion. And third, she may have been rich. Let's talk a little about each of these.*

Discussion Questions:
- Who would you say is the most famous woman from the Bible?

- Who would you say was the first person to proclaim that Jesus had been resurrected?

Allow any responses, but this question has a definitive answer: Mary Magdalene and some other women… women! A woman was the first to tell the most important news there has ever been.

Explain that even before the resurrection, this new way of life that Jesus modeled treated women differently – a whole lot better – than any religion or government had before. The apostles, Paul, and the early church continued this. The early church welcomed female members with or without their husbands, didn't treat women as property, and had women leaders and teachers. This was quite different from just about every other religion and culture.

Discussion Question:
- On whose initiative, Lydia's or God's, did Lydia become Christian?

Allow any responses, but point out the second sentence in 16:14. God acted first, opening Lydia's heart to Paul's teaching about Jesus. Affirm that Cumberland Presbyterians believe and teach that it's not our decision to repent and be saved through Christ, but doing so is our response to God's call. God can call us through the words of a teacher or preacher, through a passage of scripture, through a tugging on our hearts, through the words or actions of a friend or stranger, or any number of ways, but we always have the freedom to resist God's call and reject Christ. God acts first to invite us, and we have the choice whether or not to respond.

Discussion Question:
- Most Bible scholars believe that Lydia was rich –not Bill Gates rich, but rich compared to most everyone else who had to work hard just to survive. What do you see in her story that makes these scholars think this?

Allow any responses. Praise insightful responses. Lift up any responses about Lydia having a job, a house, or leisure time to worship.

Explain that it was unusual for a woman to be rich unless she was born to a rich father or married a rich husband. But it seems like Lydia was on her own, as no husband or father is mentioned.

Notes:

Notes:

See if anyone remembers what Jesus said about rich people. If necessary, give a hint: it has to do with a needle. "It's easier for a camel to go through the eye of a needle than for someone who is rich to enter the kingdom of God" (Matthew 19:24, Mark 10:25, Luke 18:25). Jesus didn't say rich people cannot be Christians, just that it's really hard. Lydia is proof that with hard work, self-discipline, and generosity, it's possible to have money and follow Jesus. The trick is to keep each in its proper place: Jesus with first priority, followed by money. Priorities is very important when handling money. Lydia used her wealth to offer hospitality to missionaries and to start a church in her home.

Discussion Question:
- What do you think it means when it says Lydia was a dealer in purple cloth?

Explain that the stuff to make purple dye had to be extracted from a sea snail and was hard to extract. (It comes out white, but when processed just right produces red and purple dyes.) Fabric dyed with this particular kind of dye kept its color much longer than fabric dyed other ways. Purple fabric, then, was very expensive and therefore a serious status symbol.

Discussion Question:
- What do people today wear or carry as status symbols?

Affirm that wearing purple or having purple curtains was similar back then.

Explain that the purple fabric Lydia sold was probably used for clothing by Romans and Greeks who were very rich, not at all Christian, and possibly even working against the Church. It was probably also purchased for decorating temples to the Greek and Roman gods.

Use the following questions to start and guide a discussion about faith, business, and living.

Discussion Questions:
- If Lydia made a living selling stuff to non-Christians to be used for non-Christian purposes, do you think that after she became a Christian she stopped?
    - Allow responses, but make students support their answers by asking, Why or why not?
- If she did keep her business, do you think Lydia was all churchy on Sundays, but all cutthroat business-like and money-focused the rest of the week? Why or why not?

- Would it be hard for a Christian to earn a living by dealing with non-Christians? What are some jobs today that involve helping non-Christians? Would some jobs be off-limits for a Christian? Why or why not?
- If Lydia did keep her business, what are some ways she could have lived out her faith while continuing to sell purple cloth to people who worshiped fake gods?

Now What? (20 min.)

Give each student five or six index cards and a pen. Tell them to write two or three professions or careers they might pursue on some of the cards (one per card). They are not to sign their name to the cards.

When students are done, tell them to write professions they can envision other class members pursuing on the remaining cards, but without attaching any classmates' names to the professions. Again, one profession per card.

Collect all the cards in a bag or bucket, and shake or stir them very well.

Gather students into groups of three. Even if you have a small class, make at least two groups. If you have three or fewer students, just remain in one group.

Pass out the index cards as if you're dealing playing cards, until all the cards are distributed and each group has about the same number of cards.

Instruct students to work as a team within their small groups to come up with several ways a Christian could live out his or her faith in the profession printed on each card. Have them write those suggestions on the card. These suggestions can be big things or little things, easy or hard, practical or fanciful.

For example, let's say the profession on the card is "Profes

Notes:

Notes:

sional Athlete." The small group could come up with and write some suggestions like: mention Jesus Christ in every interview, share your faith with team mates, tithe from that huge salary, publicly support Christian-based charities, start your own charity, lead the team in prayer before games.

Allow about eight to ten minutes for this activity. Roam among the groups to offer advice or suggestions… and to keep students on task. If necessary, remind students that the point of this exercise is not to figure out who wrote what, but to help each other live as Christians.

When time is up, have each group share with the whole class the profession on their cards and the suggestions they made. When the group is done with each card, have one member put the card on the bulletin board with a pushpin or on a wall with painters/masking tape. After class, whoever is interested in that profession can take the card home.

Live It (5 min.)

Say: *Lydia teaches us that accepting Christ is just the beginning of the Christian journey. Living according to Christ's plan continues the journey. Following Christ in how we live our lives every day may not be easy, and it may not be financially lucrative, but it is good, right, and pleasing to God… and nothing is more important than that.*

Encourage students to take index cards with professions they might be interested in pursuing and suggestions from their classmates about how to live as a Christian in that profession.

Resources used: Acts by William Willimon, All the Women of the Bible by Edith Deen, betterdaysarecoming.com/bible/pronunciation, The Interpreter's Bible Vol. 9

© 2014 Discipleship Ministry Team of the Ministry Council of the Cumberland Presbyterian Church. All Rights Reserved.

DIGGING DEEPER

Cumberland Presbyterians stand in the middle ground between those who say God decides who is saved and who isn't, and those who say it's fully up to us to decide whether or not we're going to accept Christ. The former position comes from a deep respect for God and God's "otherness" from us: we can't do anything to affect what God wants to happen and God is in control. The latter position comes from the belief that God loves us so much he gave us free will to choose a relationship, but God really wants us to choose salvation. Cumberland Presbyterians believe that, when we're ready to hear him, God calls us to salvation. Cumberland Presbyterians also believe that God gives us the faith to accept Christ, but we still have the freedom to choose whether or not to respond to God's call, receive that gift of faith, and accept Christ as savior. After accepting Christ as savior, we still need to make him our Lord.

That is what this lesson is about. Having a lord (or master) means doing what your lord wants, rather than what you want; going where your lord wants you to go, rather than where you want to go; earning a living in the way your lord wants, rather than how you want to. While that may not sound like a very fun or fulfilling way to live, with Christ as Lord, it is because Christ the Lord wants only the best for our lives and every life we affect. By following Christ, or making Jesus our lord, we allow the Holy Spirit to equip, empower, and lead us to a better life for ourselves, for creation, and for other people. God changing us in this way is called "sanctification." After salvation, there are two choices: sanctification (growth in grace, spiritual growth, deepening one's discipleship), or stagnation. Christians should never stop growing.

Notes:

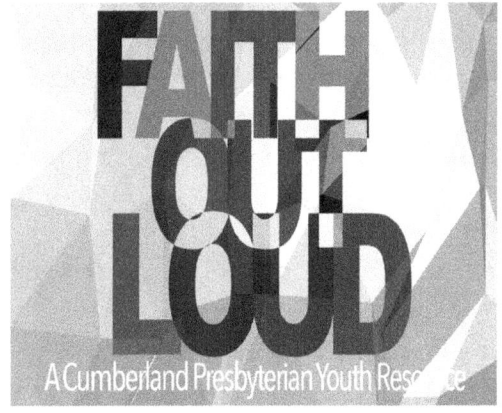

Cumberland Presbyterian Women
by Andy McClung

Scripture: Genesis 1:26-27

Theme: Many women, both lay and clergy, have done an incredible amount of ministry within, through, for, and on behalf of the Cumberland Presbyterian Church.

Resource List

- Index cards
- One of three options: Bulletin board and pushpins/ a wall and masking tape/ a piece of string, 10-15 feet long, and tape or lots of paperclips
- A coin to flip
- Stopwatch or watch/clock with a second hand
- "Her Story/Our Story" handouts
- A long-time member of your congregation

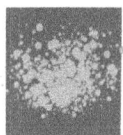

Leader Prep

- Photocopy the pages titled "Her Story/Our Story," and separate the paragraphs
- Write historical events on index cards as detailed below.

Well before class, write these significant historic events on index cards, one event per card. Do not write the date on the card. That's to use later.

- The U.S. allows states to decide voting laws. Women in every state but New Jersey lose the right to vote. (1787)
- New Jersey revokes women's right to vote. (1807)
- The Cumberland Presbyterian Church is born in Samuel McAdow's cabin. (1810)
- Wyoming (not yet a state) grants women full voting rights. (1869).
- The Colored Cumberland Presbyterian Church is formed, now the CPCA. (1874)
- Nolin Presbytery of the CP Church ordains Louisa Woosley as a minister, the first Presbyterian body to ordain a woman. (1889)
- The General Assembly of the Cumberland Presbyterian Church officially approves ordaining women as elders. (1892)
- The CPCA (then the Colored Cumberland Presbyterian Church) ordains its first female minister, Alice Bishop. (1899)
- The 19th Amendment to the U.S. Constitution becomes law, guaranteeing women the right to vote. (August 1920)

Notes:

- The General Assembly of the Cumberland Presbyterian officially approves ordaining women as ministers. (1921)
- The U.S. ends the practice of a woman losing her U.S. citizenship for marrying a citizen of another country. (1922)
- First woman elected governor of a U.S. state: Nellie Tayloe Ross, Wyoming (1925)
- Gertrude Ederly becomes first woman to swim the English Channel. (1926)
- Amelia Earhart becomes first woman to pilot an airplane across the Atlantic (1928).
- The Presbyterian Church (USA) begins ordaining women as elders. (1930)
- The Presbyterian Church (USA) ordains first female minister. (1956)
- Valentina Tereshkova becomes the first woman in space. (1963)
- Sandra Day O'Connor becomes first woman on U.S. Supreme Court. (1981)
- Geraldine Ferraro becomes first female candidate for U.S. vice-president. (1984)
- Southern Baptists stop ordaining women as pastors. (1984)
- First female elder, Beverly St. John, elected as moderator of the Cumberland Presbyterian Church's General Assembly. (1988)
- First female minister, Linda Glenn, elected as moderator of the Cumberland Presbyterian Church's General Assembly. (2005)
- Luz Dary Guerrero de Rivera becomes first Mexican female CP minister. (February 2014)
- Nobuko Seki becomes first CP female minister ordained by Japan Presbytery. (March 2014)

- Arrange for some of the long-time members of the congregation to share a little of your congregation's history with the class, focusing on significant women.

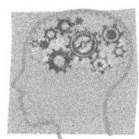

Leader Insight

Connecting to Your Students
While your students may be aware that in the past certain professions were pretty much reserved for men and others for women, they've never personally experienced a time when there weren't women in every profession. Though those days of segregating "women's work" and "men's work" really weren't very long ago, your students have never witnessed it on a grand scale. It all seems like ancient history to them and therefore is likely to be considered irrelevant. The normalcy of women in important positions may diminish teens' appreciation for women's struggles to earn those positions.

Use this lesson not only to affirm the importance of women to the CP Church, but also to celebrate the ministries of women – both lay and clergy – in our Church over the years. Future elders, ministers, chaplains, moderators, missionaries, executives, and hard workers of the CP Church sit in your classroom every week.

Explaining the Lesson
We Cumberland Presbyterians like to brag that we were the first Presbyterian body to ordain a female minister and one of the first churches in the U.S. to ordain a female minister. This is true, and certainly something to be proud of, but it does not paint a completely accurate picture of our history... or our present.

In November of 1889, Nolin Presbytery, located in Kentucky, ordained Louisa (loo-EYE-sah) Woosley as a minister in the Cumberland Presbyterian Church. This was not a spur-of-the-moment decision by Louisa or the presbytery. Louisa actually had felt God calling her to ministry many years earlier, but having seen only male ministers she figured that she must be wrong; God must not call women to be preachers. Louisa ignored this call for years. When she could no longer ignore it, she tried to avoid it or deflect it, even going so far as praying that God would call her husband into ministry. God didn't.

Eventually, Louisa even went through the whole Bible, verse-by-verse, looking for every mention of a woman to prove to herself that God doesn't call women to preach. That's what she'd heard from preachers before, basing their opinions on some of the things Paul wrote. Louisa figured that if she could prove to herself that a female minister was not in keeping

Notes:

Leader Tip:
To learn more about Louisa's story, read Shall Woman Preach, by Louisa Woosley. It's a quick, fun, and educational read.

---

with Holy Scripture, then she would be done with this sense of call to ministry. What she found in the Bible, however, was story after story that proved just the opposite. God does call women to proclaim the gospel. So, finally, after years of ignoring, avoiding, and deflecting the call, Louisa submitted to God and presented herself to her presbytery. Nolin Presbytery took her in as a candidate in the usual way and put her through the usual study and examination process. She was under the care of Nolin Presbytery for two years and proved herself to be knowledgeable of the Bible, church history, and other relevant subjects. She was also an excellent preacher and evangelist.

Then Kentucky Synod said Nolin Presbytery was wrong to ordain a woman. And when Nolin Presbytery sent Louisa as a delegate to General Assembly, there was arguing between the synod, presbytery, and General Assembly. General Assembly voted whether or not to accept her as a delegate. Seventy-eight delegates recognized her as a duly-ordained minister and therefore a legitimate delegate; eighty-five delegates, however, voted the opposite. General Assembly, then, refused to accept her as a delegate or even as a minister. When Nolin Presbytery was dissolved, Louisa transferred to Owensboro Presbytery. Kentucky Synod and General Assembly continued the argument with this presbytery. While all this arguing was going on, more presbyteries were accepting women as candidates for ordination, and some congregations began electing and ordaining women as elders. It wasn't until 1921, the year following women gaining the right to vote across the U.S., that General Assembly finally stopped trying to keep women out of the ministry.

So the sanitized version of the story says we Cumberland Presbyterian have been ordaining women since 1889, but the whole story isn't very neat or very nice.

Most of our presbyteries today will accept women as candidates for ordination with no fuss. That's the sanitized version of the present story. The uglier reality comes into play when those women have spent years of their lives and lots of their dollars gaining an education to meet the requirements for ordination… and then find that very few congregations are willing to call a woman to be the pastor. This is getting better than it has been in years past, but a woman still has far fewer choices than a man.

Many Cumberland Presbyterian women seeking ordination end up going into some kind of chaplaincy, or Christian education position—all perfectly valid and important ministries, but not completely fulfilling when they come as a second or third choice.

Some CP congregations still refuse to elect women as elders. Some CP congregations won't even consider calling a woman to be the pastor. Yet in all of these congregations, there are women doing lots of ministry.

For the last several years, the percentage of CP ministers who are women has steadily remained around ten percent. That's not counting persons preparing for ordination, just ordained clergy. Look at the membership of any CP congregation, though; it's likely that there are at least as many women as men active in the church – probably more – and it's equally likely that much of the ministry of that congregation is done by women. When we look back, we see an incredible amount of ministry has been done by women over the years, and this continues on today.

Theological Underpinnings

In Genesis 1:26, God says, "Let us make humankind in our image." Then Genesis 1:27 tells us that God did exactly that: "So God created humankind in his image, in the image of God he created them; male and female he created them." That's how the NRSV words it. Other translations of the Bible use different words in place of "humankind" – "man" (KJV, ESV, NASB); "human beings" (NCV, GNT); "mankind" (NIV). All these words mean the same thing: humans as a species. The Hebrew word originally used here was "adam," which means "man" as a species. In English, "man" was once used to indicate all of humanity. Since that word can be ambiguous and lead to confusion, today there's no reason not to use the more clear "humankind."

Our Confession of Faith draws from Genesis to conclude, "God is the creator of all ... only human beings are created in God's own image. In the sight of God, male and female are created equal and complementary." (1.10-1.11) So, with Holy Scripture and our own doctrine affirming that men and women are created equal, the only reason not to support women in ministry has to come from some other source, a source that's not God-inspired. (Some denominations say that God gave women and men different roles, and preaching is a role reserved for men.)

A frequent response to the question about openness to women in ministry is, "I'm not personally opposed to a fe-

Notes:

male pastor, but some people in my congregation are." This response is sometimes used by members of pastor search committees. At best, it's an excuse not to consider qualified women in the search. At worst, it's a lie. Not every minister, regardless of gender, is suited for every congregation, but many CP congregations have missed out on a potentially long and fruitful relationship with a pastor just because they wouldn't consider a woman in their search. Chances are, though, that these very same congregations have women doing valuable ministry anyway: teaching Sunday school, leading worship by playing the piano or singing, serving in the choir, raising money, doing mission projects, caring for children in the nursery, cleaning the building, bringing visitors to worship, promoting the congregation to the community with positive comments, witnessing at their jobs, and more.

Applying the Lesson to Your Own Life
Recall some of the women who have been good influences in your spiritual life. Thank God for them.

Think of the best church workers you've known: the most gifted Sunday school teachers, most dedicated church members, most sincere prayer warriors, the first with a card or call or hug at critical times. Chances are that you just thought of more women than men.

Do you support women in ministry? How? What more can you do? Would it surprise you to know that just as many women as men are opposed to women ministers? Why do you think that is?

If you were serving on a pastor search committee, would you give equal consideration to potential pastors, regardless of gender? Why or why not?

Does your congregation have CPWM? If so, how much of their focus is on doing ministry for those outside the congregation? Did you know these groups got their start focusing on international missions?

The Lesson

Get Started (10 min.)

Divide students by gender, even if it means one person on a team. Try to make this division seem random, if possible. ("Okay, we need two teams... let's see... hmmm... how about girls vs. boys this time?")

Have each team designate an official answerer.

Explain that you are going to ask each team a series of questions. You can only take an answer from the official answerer, and you must take the first answer that person gives you.

Each correct answer earns the team one point. The team with the most points at the end of the game wins. A tie stands as is; there is no tie-breaker. No technology other than students' brains is allowed to find answers.

Flip a coin to see which team goes first. Ask the questions below to the team indicated, alternating between teams with each question. Give each team 20 seconds to answer. You can use a stopwatch, or have students time the opposing team using stopwatch apps on their phones. Repeat the question upon request, but only once. Teams can discuss their answers and instruct their answerer how to answer, but the official answer is the one the answerer gives you first.

If a team gives the wrong answer or runs out of time before answering, they get no point, but be sure to allow the opposing team to reveal that they know the correct answer.
Keep track of correct answers, maybe by circling the question number.

Questions for the Girls:
1. Is a chainsaw more likely to have a two-stroke engine or a four-stroke engine? (Answer: two)
2. Is WD-40 a football play, a type of gun, a lubricant, or map coordinates? (Answer: a lubricant)
3. Rank these poker hands from highest to lowest: full house, straight flush, four of a kind. (Answer: straight flush, four of a kind, full house)
4. How many points is a touchdown worth? (Answer: 6)

Notes:

Notes:

5. What is Jim Bowie famous for: his hat, his knife, his car, or his poetry? (Answer: knife)
6. Rainbow, brown, and brook are types of what: hunting bows, boats, turkey, or trout. (Answer: trout)
7. Which martial art did Bruce Lee develop: Aikido, Taekwondo, Jeet Kune Do, or Krav Maga? (Answer: Jeet Kune Do)
8. Who won the first Super Bowl: Kansas City Chiefs, Mianmi Dolphins, Green Bay Packers, or Oakland raiders? (Answer: Green Bay Packers)
9. Which of these types of ammunition is primarily for a rifle: .38 Special, .44 magnum, .223, or 9 millimeter? (Answer: .223)
10. Where's the best place to hold a hammer: as close to the head as possible, at the bottom of the handle, in the middle of the handle, it depends on what kind of nail you're driving. (Answer: at the bottom of the handle)

Questions for the Boys:

1. What do you do with an orangewood stick: eat it, clean under your nails with it, exfoliate with it, apply makeup with it, or plant it? (Answer: clean under your nails with it)
2. Which one doesn't belong: platforms, flats, spike, wedges? (Answer: flats)
3. What do you call a swimsuit that's a cross between a one-piece and a two-piece? (Answer: Tankini)
4. Are concealer and foundation the same thing? (Answer: no)
5. Name two kinds of liner used in makeup. (Answer: lip liner and eye liner)
6. What color is a Sterling Silver Rose: violet, silver, red, or pink? (Answer: violet)
7. Who wrote the book Little Women: Emily Bronte, Louisa May Alcott, Laura Ingalls Wilder, or Charlotte Bronte? (Answer: Louisa May Alcott)
8. If a girl said she wanted a Perrier, what is she asking for? (Answer: French sparkling water)
9. Which of these is a not a brand of shoes: Gucci, Terrence Witbier, Jimmy Choo, or Brian Atwood? (Answer: Terrence Witbier)
10. Who wrote the Twilight series: J.K. Rowling, Stephanie Meyer, Anne Rice, Patricia Cornwell? (Answer: Stephanie Meyer)

Total up the scores, announce the winning team, allow a moment for bragging, and then say something like:

There are some things most girls can usually do better than most guys, and there are some things most guys can do better than most girls. There are some things most guys know more about than most girls, and there are some things most girls know more about than most guys. And then there are a lot of things where gender doesn't matter.

Ministry is one of those things where gender doesn't matter. God calls every Christian to minister according to their gifts, abilities, and opportunities. God calls some men and women to become ordained ministers. The Cumberland Presbyterian Church affirms and supports both men and women in all kinds of ministry.

 ## Listen Up (20 min.)

Gather the index cards prepared with the following information.
- The U.S. allows states to decide voting laws. Women in every state but New Jersey lose the right to vote. (1787)
- New Jersey revokes women's right to vote. (1807)
- The Cumberland Presbyterian Church is born in Samuel McAdow's cabin. (1810)
- Wyoming (not yet a state) grants women full voting rights. (1869).
- The Colored Cumberland Presbyterian Church is formed, now the CPCA. (1874)
- Nolin Presbytery of the CP Church ordains Louisa Woosley as a minister, the first Presbyterian body to ordain a woman. (1889)
- The General Assembly of the Cumberland Presbyterian Church officially approves ordaining women as elders. (1892)
- The CPCA (then the Colored Cumberland Presbyterian Church) ordains its first female minister, Alice Bishop. (1899)
- The 19th Amendment to the U.S. Constitution becomes law, guaranteeing women the right to vote. (August 1920)
- The General Assembly of the Cumberland Presbyte-

Notes:

Notes:

rian officially approves ordaining women as ministers. (1921)
- The U.S. ends the practice of a woman losing her U.S. citizenship for marrying a citizen of another country. (1922)
- First woman elected governor of a U.S. state: Nellie Tayloe Ross, Wyoming (1925)
- Gertrude Ederly becomes first woman to swim the English Channel. (1926)
- Amelia Earhart becomes first woman to pilot an airplane across the Atlantic (1928).
- The Presbyterian Church (USA) begins ordaining women as elders. (1930)
- The Presbyterian Church (USA) ordains first female minister. (1956)
- Valentina Tereshkova becomes the first woman in space. (1963)
- Sandra Day O'Connor becomes first woman on U.S. Supreme Court. (1981)
- Geraldine Ferraro becomes first female candidate for U.S. vice-president. (1984)
- Southern Baptists stop ordaining women as pastors. (1984)
- First female elder, Beverly St. John, elected as moderator of the Cumberland Presbyterian Church's General Assembly. (1988)
- First female minister, Linda Glenn, elected as moderator of the Cumberland Presbyterian Church's General Assembly. (2005)
- Luz Dary Guerrero de Rivera becomes first Mexican female CP minister. (February 2014)
- Nobuko Seki becomes first CP female minister ordained by Japan Presbytery. (March 2014)

Have someone in the class read Genesis 1:26-27. For clarity, use a translation of the Bible that uses "humankind" or "human beings" rather than "man."

Say: *God intended men and women to be equal, but that hasn't always been the case.*

Use the index cards you prepared to play a game with your students. Two options are possible.

Option #1
Give each student one or more cards, and have them arrange the cards chronologically as best they can determine. Choose your most talkative student – the one always first to

venture forth with an answer or opinion, the one most likely to tell others what to do – and make him/her the "poster child." This person's job is to remain silent and "post" the cards in the order the others students say. Cards may be stuck to a bulletin board with pushpins, or taped to a wall. Don't make this a "beat the clock" game, but don't let it drag on forever either.

Option #2
Choose 2 to 5 of your most talkative students—the ones always first to venture forth with an answer or opinion, the ones most likely to tell others what to do. Have these students hold the string – one on either end, and the others evenly spaced in between – and give them instructions to stay silent. Give the index cards to the remaining students, and tell them to tape or paperclip them onto the string in chronological order as best they can determine.

For either option, students should work together to determine the correct chronological order. This should involve discussing, debating, and compromising. Offer some hints here and there, if necessary. Be sure to remind your string holders or poster child to remain silent, even if they're asked a question by another student. Overall, though, this is one of those exercises where you should be as involved as little as possible. Let the students take charge and do most of the work.

When students think they have the cards in order, reveal the correct order of the historic events. Have a student or two make corrections as you go. When you're done, tape the string to a hallway wall or somewhere else the whole congregation can see it.

Discussion Questions:
- Did we do better or worse than you thought we would?
- Was there anything that happened a lot earlier or later than you would have thought?
- Were there any other surprises?
- Which of these events did you already know about?
- Which of these events do you want to know more about?
- (To just the string holders or poster child) Did you know some of the things they got wrong? What was it like having to remain silent, having no power to influence what was going on?

Allow responses to that last question, then say something like: It wasn't pleasant or fair for him/her/them to be silenced,

Notes:

Notes:

but that's exactly what women had to endure for many years, both in society and in the church.

Now What? (15 min.)

Well before class, arrange for one or two of the long-time members of your congregation to visit the last portion of the class meeting. Ask them to share some stories of the women who were influential in the life of your congregation. The older these guests are and the longer they've been part of the congregation, the better. If you know of a homebound member who can tell some good stories, consider arranging a visit and recording a video. Then show the video to your students during this part of class.

Before these visitors arrive, coach your students to be patient and respectful. Inviting grandparents of your students, if they're members, may help with this.

Also before class, photocopy the pages below labeled "Her Story/Our Story," and use scissors to separate the paragraphs.

In class, distribute the "Her Story/Our Story" paragraphs among your students. Have students, in no particular order, stand and read their paragraph.

When all Her Story/Our Story information has been shared, say: *God doesn't expect everyone to be a superstar in the Church, but God does expect each of us – male or female – to do ministry according to our gifts, resources, and opportunities. Each of those women we just heard about was, at some point, a member of a Cumberland Presbyterian congregation. Now let's hear about some of the women from this congregation.*

Introduce your guests, the long-time members of your congregation.

If any of the long-time members you bring to the classroom are women, wait until they have shared stories of other women important to the congregation's history, and then ask them to tell about some of the things they have done in the church.

Live It (5 min.)

Close the lesson with the following, or a similar prayer: *Thank you, God, for all the women who have found a place to serve you and others in the Cumberland Presbyterian Church. Use us in this room to help this denomination continue to affirm and support women in doing ministry of all kinds.*

Resources used: A People Called Cumberland Presbyterian, by Ben Barrus and others, cumberland.org, dpsinfo.com, religioustolerance.org, Shall Woman Preach, by Louisa Woosley

© 2014 Discipleship Ministry Team of the Ministry Council of the Cumberland Presbyterian Church. All Rights Reserved.

DIGGING DEEPER

For more about women in ministry, get the Faith Out Loud lesson entitled, "Can Preachers Wear High Heels?"

Her Story/Our Story

Her Story/Our Story: REV. LOUISA (loo-EYE-sah) WOOSLEY was the first woman to become an ordained minister in the CP Church. That was in 1889. She not only paved the way for other female ministers, but she also pastored churches and preached thousands of times at revivals. Many people came to know Jesus through her preaching.

Her Story/Our Story: JOHNNIE MASSEY CLAY became president of an almost nonexistent Women's Board of Missions in 1916, and served for 20 years. She got the denomination excited about carrying the gospel beyond the U.S. She organized fundraisers to raise incredible amounts of money to support missionaries. And everyone knew her to be a person who prayed for mission work all the time.

Her Story/Our Story: BERNICE BARNETT GONZALEZ and ETHEL BRINTLE went to Colombia, South America in 1928, to help with the denomination's mission work there. They soon learned that the Spanish they learned in school was almost worthless, but they persevered and were vital in making this one of our most successful international missionary efforts.

Her Story/Our Story: AMERICA DRENNAN, a widow, responded to a request from our first missionaries in Japan who were seeking help to establish a girls' school there. In 1883, she gave $3,000 (equivalent to $74,000 today). She also moved to Japan, learned the language, adopted two children, and did an enormous amount of mission work during her 20 years there.

Her Story/Our Story: CLAUDETTE PICKLE was an elementary school teacher before she focused her education in education on the CP Church. She served as the denominational Coordinator of Children's Ministry for 16 years and then the Executive Director of the Board of Christian Education for 17 years. Her 2009 retirement didn't stop her ministry, though. She became the director of Christian education in a local CP congregation.

Her Story/Our Story

Her Story/Our Story: CORNELIA SWAIN faithfully worked in local and denominational women's ministries from 1977 until 2002.

Her Story/Our Story: REV. MARGARET McKEE was ordained in 1979, and served for many years as a hospital chaplain, comforting the sick, praying with patients and their families, spiritually advising hospital staff, and helping people in need find peace.

Her Story/Our Story: EDITH OLD was director of a nonprofit company that cared for blind persons and their families. In 2008, she became the first person to be the Director of Ministries of the Cumberland Presbyterian Church. This newly formed position was part of a complete overhaul of our denominational leadership's structure. Many thought a minster should be in this position, but Edith has proved that it's not just ministers who can provide dedicated leadership in doing ministry.

Her Story/Our Story: After REV. LOUISA WOOSLEY paved the way in 1889, five more women became Cumberland Presbyterian ministers before it was officially legal. They were REV. BESSIE MORRIS in 1907, REV. MABELLE ROBINSON in 1917, BIRDIE LEE PALLETTEE in 1916, REV. CHLOE KRATLI in 1919, and ADA SLATON in 1920.

Her Story/Our Story: REV. LISA ANDERSON served for twenty years as a chaplain at St. Jude Children's Research Hospital, ministering to countless children dealing with cancer and treatment for it. When she left St. Jude in 2013, she revitalized an almost-dead congregation by helping the congregation shift its focus from taking care of its own members to ministering to the homeless, impoverished, and at-risk persons in the community.

Her Story/Our Story: REV. DR. TIFFANY HALL McCLUNG became the first full-time chaplain at Memphis Theological Seminary in 2008. She plans and leads weekly worship services for the seminary community, while ministering to the needs of students, staff, and faculty.

About the contributors...

Rev. Melissa Goodloe earned her M. Div. (05) at Memphis Theological Seminary. Rev. Goodloe is the pastor of the Shiloh CP Church, McKenzie, Tennessee. She and her husband Tim reside in the Macedonia community with their 2 dogs, 2 cats, and a school of fish.

Rev. Dr. Andy McClung has been teaching Cumberland Presbyterian youth and adults since 1988, both in person and through his writing. A double graduate of Memphis Theological Seminary (M.Div., 1994 and D.Min., 2002), Andy has served congregations in Alabama, Arkansas, Mississippi, and Tennessee. Cursed with a dry sense of humor and blessed with a love for the Cumberland Presbyterian Church, he lives in Memphis and continues to teach, preach, write, and serve the church at the presbyterial, synodic, and denominational levels.

Abby Prevost is originally from Columbus, Mississippi, and is currently serving in youth ministry at the Flat Lick CP Church in Hopkinsville, Kentucky. She has a bachelor's degree in Human Services and Sociology from Bethel University and is a student at Memphis Theological Seminary pursing a degree in a Masters of Arts in Youth Ministry through the Center for Youth Ministry Training Program.

Rev. Chris Warren has served in many capacities in the Cumberland Presbyterian Church including leading music and working with youth at local, presbytery, and denominational events. He is senior pastor at the Murfreesboro Cumberland Presbyterian Church in Murfreesboro, Tennessee. Chris and his beautiful wife, Joy, have two wonderful children, Emma and Micah.

Taylor Young is currently attending Memphis Theological Seminary and training in youth ministry with the Center for Youth Ministry Training and serving a church in youth ministry through the program. He has a Bachelors in Social Work from Middle Tennessee State University. Taylor is also a candidate for the ministry in Nashville Presbytery.

Series editor for *Faith Out Loud* is Susan Guin Groce. Line editor is Mark A. Taylor. Electronic processing and incidental layout by Matthew H. Gore. *Faith Out Loud* logo and cover design are by Joanna Bellis. Produced for the Discipleship Ministry Team of the Ministry Council of the Cumberland Presbyterian Church.